THE BUDDHIST CATECHISM

THE
BUDDHIST CATECHISM

BY

HENRY S. OLCOTT

RESIDENT-FOUNDER OF THE THEOSOPHICAL SOCIETY

Approved and recommended for use in Buddhist Schools by* H. SUMANGALA, *Pradhana Nyaaka Sthavira,High Priest of Sripada and the Western Province and principal of the Vidyodaya Pirivena

ISBN: 978-93-5128-803-9(HB)

First Published in 1903
Indian Reprint in 2017

Published by

Kalpaz Publications
C-30, Satyawati Nagar,
Delhi – 110052
E-mail: kalpaz@hotmail.com
Website: kalpazpublications.com
Ph.: +91-9212142040

Cataloging in Publication Data—DK
Courtesy: D.K. Agencies (P) Ltd. <docinfo@dkagencies.com>

Olcott, Henry Steel, 1832-1907, **author.**
The Buddhist catechism / by Henry S. Olcott.
pages cm
"First published in 1903"—Title page verso.
"Approved and recommended for use in Buddhist schools by H. Sumangala ..."
ISBN 9789351288039

1. Buddhism—Catechisms. I. Title.

BQ4170.O43 2017 DDC 294.3927 23

DEDICATION

IN token of respect and affection I dedicate to my counsellor and friend of many years, Hikkaduwe Sumangala, Praḍhāna Nāyaka Sṭhavira and High Priest of Adam's Peak (Sripaḍa) and the Western Province, THE BUḌḌHIST CATECHISM, in its revised form.

H. S. OLCOTT.

ADYAR, 1903.

PREFACE

TO THE THIRTY-THIRD EDITION

IN the working out of my original plan, I have added more questions and answers in the text of each new English edition of the Catechism, leaving it to its translators to render them in to whichever of the other vernaculars they may be working in. The unpretending aim in view is to give so succinct and yet comprehensive a digest of Buḍḍhistic history, ethics and philosophy as to enable beginners to understand and appreciate the noble ideal taught by the Buḍḍha, and thus make it easier for them to follow out the Ḍharma in its details. In the present edition a great many new questions and answers have been introduced, while the matter has been grouped within five categories, *viz.* : (1) The Life of the Buḍḍha ; (2) the Doctrine ; (3) the Saṅgha, or monastic order ; (4) a brief history of Buḍḍhism, its Councils and propaganda ; (5) some reconciliation of Buḍḍhism with science. This, it is believed, will largely increase the value of the little book, and make it even more suitable for use in Buḍḍhist schools, of which, in Ceylon, over one hundred have already been opened by the Sinhalese people under the general supervision of the Theosophical Society. In preparing this edition I have received valuable help from some of my oldest and best qualified Sinhalese colleagues. The original edition was gone over with me word by word, by that eminent scholar and bhikkhu, H. Sumangala, Praḍhāna Nāyaka, and the Assistant Principal of his Pālī College at Colombo, Heyantuduve Anunayaka Terunnanse ;

and the High Priest has also kindly scrutinised the present revision and given me invaluable points to embody. It has the merit, therefore, of being a fair presentation of the Buḍḍhism of the "Southern Church," chiefly derived from first-hand sources. The Catechism has been published in twenty languages, mainly by Buḍḍhists, for Buḍḍhists.

H. S. O.

ADYAR, 17*th May*, 1897.

CERTIFICATE TO THE FIRST EDITION

VIḌYOḌAYA COLLEGE,
Colombo, 7th July, 1881.

I HEREBY certify that I have carefully examined the Sinhalese version of the Catechism prepared by Colonel H. S. Olcott, and that the same is in agreement with the Canon of the Southern Buḍḍhist Church. I recommend the work to teachers in Buḍḍhist schools, and to all others who may wish to impart information to beginners about the essential features of our religion.

H. SUMANGALA,
High Priest of Sripaḍa and Galle, and Principal of the Viḍyoḍaya Pirivena.

VIḌYOḌAYA COLLEGE,
April 7, 1897.

I HAVE gone over the thirty-third (English) edition of the Catechism, with the help of interpreters, and confirm my recommendation for its use in Buḍḍhist schools;

H. SUMANGALA

PREFACE

TO THE FORTIETH EDITION

THE popularity of this little work is proved by the constant demand for new editions, in English and other languages. In looking over the matter for the present edition, I have found very little to change or to add, for the work seems to present a very fair idea of the contents of Southern Buḍḍhism ; and, as my object is never to write an extended essay on the subject, I resist the temptation to wander off into amplifications of details which, however interesting to the student of comparative religion, are useless in a rational scheme of elementary instruction.

The new Sinhalese version (38th edition) which is being prepared by my respected friend, D. B. Jayaṭilaka, Principal of Ānanḍa (Buḍḍhist) College, Colombo, is partly printed, but cannot be completed until he is relieved of some of the pressure upon his time. The Tamil version (41st edition) has been undertaken by the leaders of the Pañchama community of Madras, and will shortly issue from the press. The Spanish version (39th edition) is in the hands of my friend, Señor Xifré, and the French one (37th edition) in those of Commandant Courmes.

I am afraid we shall have to wait long for this help to come from the Buḍḍhist bhikkhus, almost the only learned men of Ceylon ; at least I have not been able during an intimate intercourse of twenty-two years, to arouse their zeal. It has always seemed to me incongruous that an American, making no claims at all to scholarship, should be looked to by the Sinhalese to help them teach the ḍharma to their children ; and as I believe I have said in an earlier edition, I only consented to write THE BUḌḌHIST CATECHISM after I had found that no bhikkhu would undertake it. Whatever its demerits, I can at least say that the work contains the essence of some 15,000 pages of Buḍḍhist teaching that I have read in connexion with my work.

H. S. O.

ADYAR,
7th February, 1903.

PREFACE

TO THE FORTY-SECOND EDITION

THE writer of this Catechism has passed away from earth, but, before he left the body, he had arranged with the High Priest Sumangala to make some small corrections in the text. These are incorporated in the present edition by the High Priest's wish, expressed to me in Colombo, in November, 1907.

I have not altered the numbering of the questions as it might cause confusion in a class to change the numbers, if some pupils had the older editions and some the new.

ANNIE BESANT.

ADYAR,
17th February, 1908.

PREFACE

TO THE THIRTY-SIXTH EDITION

THE popularity of this little work seems undiminished, edition after edition being called for. While the present one was in the press a second German edition, re-translated by the learned Dr. Erich Bischoff, was published at Leipzig, by the Griebens Co., and a third translation into French, by my old friend and colleague, Commandant D. A. Courmes, was being got ready at Paris. A fresh version, in Sinhalese is also preparing at Colombo. It is very gratifying to a declared Buḍḍhist like myself to read what so ripe a scholar as Mr. G. R. S. Mead, author of *Fragments of a Faith Forgotten*, *Pistis Sophia*, and many other works on Christian origins, thinks of the value of the compilation. He writes in the *Theosophical Review*: "It has been translated into no less than twenty different languages, and may be said without the faintest risk of contradiction, to have been the busiest instrument of Buḍḍhist propaganda for many a day in the annals of that long somnolent ḍharma. The least that learned Buḍḍhists of Ceylon can do to repay the debt of gratitude they owe to Colonel Olcott and, other members of the Theosophical Society who have worked for them, is to bestir themselves to throw some light on their own origins and doctrines."

So the work goes on, and by this unpretending agency the teachings of the Buḍḍha Ḍharma are being carried throughout the world.

H. S. O.

ADYAR, *7th January*, 1905.

CONTENTS

THE BUDDHIST CATECHISM

PART I

THE LIFE OF THE BUDDHA

1. Question. *Of what religion[1] are you?*

Answer. The Buḍḍhist.

---

[1]The word "religion" is most inappropriate to apply to Buḍḍhism which is not a religion, but a moral philosophy, as I have shown later on. But by common usage the word has been applied to all groups of people who profess a special moral doctrine, and is so employed by statisticians. The Sinhalese Buḍḍhists have never yet had any conception of what Europeans imply in the etymological construction of the Latin root of this term. In their creed there is no such thing as a "binding" in the Christian sense—a submission to or merging of self in a Divine Being. *Āgama* is their vernacular word to express their relation to Buḍḍhism and the BUḌḌHA. It is pure Samskrṭ, and means "approach, or coming"; and as "*Buḍḍha*" is enlightenment, the compound word by which they indicate Buḍḍhism—*Buḍḍhāgama*—would be properly rendered as "an approach or coming to enlightenment," or possibly as a following of the Doctrine of SĀKYAMUNI. The missionaries, finding *Āgama* ready to their hand, adopted it as the equivalent for "religion"; and Christianity is written by them *Christianāgama*, whereas it should be *Christianibanḍhana*, for *banḍhana* is the etymological equivalent for "religion". The name *Vibhajja vāḍī*—one who analyses —is another name given to a Buḍḍhist, and *Adbayurāḍī* is a third. With this explanation, I continue to employ under protest the familiar word when speaking of Buḍḍhistic philosophy, for the convenience of the ordinary reader.

2. Q. *What is Buḍḍhism ?*

A. It is a body of teachings given out by the great personage known as the Buḍḍha.

3. Q. *Is "Buḍḍhism" the best name for this teaching ?*

A. No ; that is only a western term : the best name for it is Bauḍḍha Ḍharma.

4. Q. *Would you call a person a Buḍḍhist who had merely been born of Buḍḍhist parents ?*

A. Certainly not. A Buḍḍhist is one who not only professes belief in the Buḍḍha as the noblest of Teachers, in the Doctrine preached by Him, and in the Brotherhood of Arhaṭs, but practises His precepts in daily life.

5. Q. *What is a male lay Buḍḍhist called ?*

A. An Upāsaka.

6. Q. *What a female ?*

A. An Upāsikā.

7. Q. *When was this doctrine first preached ?*

A. There is some disagreement as to the actual date, but accoıding to the Sinhalese Scriptures it was in the year 2513 of the (present) Kali-Yuga.

8. Q. *Give the important dates in the last birth of the Founder ?*

A. He was born under the constellation Visā on a Tuesday in May, in the year 2478 (K.Y.) ; he retired to the jungle in the year 2506 ; became Buḍḍha in 2513 ; and, passing out of the round of re-births, entered Paranirvāṇa in the year 2558, aged eighty years. Each of these events happened on a day of full moon, so all are conjointly celebrated in the great festival of the full-moon of the oronth Wesak *Vaisākha*) corresponding to the month of May.

9. Q. *Was the Buḍḍha God ?*

A. No. Buḍḍha Ḍharma teaches no "divine" incarnation.

10. Q. *Was he a man ?*

A. Yes ; but the wisest, noblest and most holy being, who had developed himself in the course of countless births far beyond all other beings, the previous BUḌḌHAS alone excepted.

11. Q. *Were there other Buḍḍhas before him ?*

A. Yes ; as will be explained later on.

12. Q. *Was Buḍḍha his name ?*

A. No. It is the name of a condition or state of mind, of the mind after it has reached the culmination of development.

13. Q. *What is its meaning ?*

A. Enlightened ; or, he who has the all-perfect wisdom. The Pāli phrase is *Sabbannu*, the One of Boundless Knowledge. In Samskṛṭ it is *Sarvajña.*

14. Q. *What was the Buḍḍha's real name then ?*

A. SIDDHARTHA was his royal name, and GAUTAMA, or GOTAMA, his family name. He was Prince of Kapilavāsṭu and belonged to the illustrious family of the Okkāka, of the Solar race.

15. Q. *Who were his father and mother ?*

A. King Suḍḍhoḍana and Queen Māyā, called Mahā Māyā.

16. Q. *What people did this King reign over ?*

A. The Sākyas ; and Āryan tribe of Kṣhaṭṭriyas.

17. Q. *Where was Kapilavāsṭu ?*

A. In India, one hundred miles north-east of the City of Benares, and about forty miles from the Himālaya mountains. It is situated in the Nepāl Terai. The city is now in ruins.

18. Q. *On what river ?*

A. The Rohiṇī, now called the Rohana.

19. Q. *Tell me again when Prince Siḍḍhārṭha was born ?*

A. Six hundred and twenty-three years before the Christian era.

20. Q. *Is the exact spot known ?*

A. It is now identified beyond question. An archaeologist in the service of the Government of India has discovered in the jungle of the Nepāl Terai a stone pillar erected by the mighty Buḍḍhist sovereign, Asoka, to mark the very spot. The place was known in those times as the Lumbīni Garden.

21. Q. *Had the Prince luxuries and splendours like other Princes ?*

A. He had ; his father, the King, built him three magnificient palaces—for the three Indian seasons —the cold, the hot, and the rainy—of nine, five, and three stories respectively, and handsomely decorated.

22. Q. *How were they situated ?*

A. Around each palace were gardens of the most beautiful and fragrant flowers, with fountains of spouting water, the trees full of singing birds, and peacocks strutting over the ground.

23. Q. *Was he living alone ?*

A. No ; in his sixteenth year he was married to the Princess Yasoḍharā, daughter of the King Suprabuḍḍha. Many beatuiful maidens, skilled in dancing and music, were also in continual attendance to amuse him.

24. Q. *How did he get his wife ?*

A. In the ancient Kṣhaṭṭriya or warrior fashion, by overcoming all competitiors in games and exercises of skill and prowess, and then selecting, Yasoḍharā out of all the young princesses, whose fathers had brought them to the tournament or *mela.*

25. Q. *How, amid all this luxury, could a Prince become all-wise ?*

A. He had such natural wisdom that when but a child he seemed to understand all arts and sciences almost without study. He had the best teachers, but they could teach him nothing that he did not seem to comprehend immediately.

26. Q. *Did he become Buḍḍha in his splendid palaces ?*

A. No. He left all and went alone into the jungle.

27. Q. *Why did he do this ?*

A. To discover the cause of our sufferings and the way to escape from them.

28. Q. *Was it not selfishness that made him do this ?*

A. No ; it was boundless love for all beings that made him devote himself to their good.

29. Q. *But how did he acquire this boundless love ?*

A. Throughout numberless births and aeons of years he had been cultivating this love, with the unfaltering determination to become a Buḍḍha.

30. Q. *What did he this time relinquish ?*

A. His beautiful palaces, his riches, luxuries and pleasures, his soft beds, fine dresses, rich food, and his kingdom ; he even left his beloved wife and only son, Rāhula.

31. Q. *Did any other man ever sacrifice so much for our sake ?*

A. Not one in this present world-period : this is why Buddhists so love him, and why good Buḍḍhists try to be like him.

32. Q. *But have not many men given up all earthly blessings, and even life itself, for the sake of their fellow-men ?*

A. Certainly. But we believe that this surpassing unselfishness and love for humanity showed themselves in his renouncing the bliss of Nirvāṇa countless ages ago, when he was born as the Brāhmaṇa Sumeḍha, in the time of Ḍīpāṇkara Buḍḍha : he had then reached the stage where he might have entered Nirvāṇa, had he not loved mankind more than himself. This renunciation implied his voluntarily enduring the miseries of earthly lives until he became Buḍḍha, for the sake of teaching all beings the way to emancipation and to give rest to the world.

33. Q. *How old was he when he went to the jungle ?*

A. He was in his twenty-ninth year.

34. Q. *What finally determined him to leave all that men usually love so much and go to the jungle ?*

A. A Ḍeva[1] appeared to him when driving out in his chariot, under four impressive forms, on four different occasions.

35. Q. *What were these different forms ?*

A. Those of a very old man broken down by age, of a sick man, of a decaying corpse, and of a dignified hermit.

36. Q. *Did he alone see these ?*

A. No, his attendant, Channa, also saw them.

37. Q. *Why should these sights, so familiar to everybody, have caused him to go to the jungle ?*

A. We often see such sights : he had not seen them, so they made a deep impression on his mind.

38. Q. *Why had he not also seen them ?*

A. The Brāhmaṇa astrologers had foretold at his birth that he would one day resign his kingdom and become a BUḌḌHA. The King, his father, not wishing to lose an heir to his kingdom, had carefully prevented his seeing any sights that might suggest to him

[1] See the definition of *ḍeva* given later.

human misery and death. No one was allowed even to speak of such things to the Prince. He was almost like a prisoner in his lovely palaces and flower gardens. They were surrounded by high walls, and inside everything was made as beautiful as possible, so that he might not wish to go and see the sorrow and distress that are in the world.

39. Q. *Was he so kind-hearted that the King feared he might really wish to leave everything for the world's sake* ?

A. Yes ; he seems to have felt for all beings so strong a pity and love as that.

40. Q. *And how did he expect to learn the cause of sorrow in the jungle* ?

A. By removing far away from all that could prevent his thinking deeply of the causes of sorrow and the nature of man.

41. Q. *How did he escape from the palace* ?

A. One night, when all were asleep, he arose, took a last look at his sleeping wife and infant son ; called Channa, mounted his favourite white horse Kanthaka, and rode to the palace gate. The *Ḍevas* had thrown a deep sleep upon the King's guard who watched the gate, so that they could not hear the noise of the horse's hoofs.

42. Q. *But the gate was locked, was it not* ?

A. Yes ; but the *Ḍevas* caused it to open without the slightest noise, and he rode away into the darkness.

43. Q. *Whither did he go ?*

A. To the river Anomā, a long way from, Kapilavāsṭu.

44. Q. *What did he then do ?*

A. He sprang from his horse, cut off his beautiful hair with his sword, put on the yellow dress of an ascetic, and giving his ornaments and horse to Channa, ordered him to take them back to his father the King.

45. Q. *What then ?*

A. He went afoot towards Rājagṛaha, the capital city of King Bimbisāra, of Magaḍha.

46. Q. *Who visited him there ?*

A. The King with his whole Court.[1]

46*a*. Q. *Thence whither did he go ?*

A. To Uruvela, near the present Mahābōḍhi Temple at Buḍḍha Gayā.

47. Q. *Why did he go there ?*

A. In the forests were hermits—very wise men, whose pupil he afterwards became, in the hope of finding the knowledge of which he was in search.

48. Q. *Of what religion were they ?*

A. The Hinḍū religion : they were Brāhmaṇas[2].

---

[1] For an admirable account of this interview consult Dr. Paul Carus' *Gospel of Buḍḍha*, page 20, *et seq.*

[2] The term Hindu, once a contemptuous term, used by the Musalmans to designate the people of Sindh, whom they conquered, is now used in an ecclesiastical sense.

49. Q. *What did they teach ?*

A. That by severe penances and torture of the body a man may acquire perfect wisdom.

50. Q. *Did the Prince find this to be so ?*

A. No ; he learned their systems and practised all their penances, but he could not thus discover the cause of human sorrow and the way to absolute emancipation.

51. Q. *What did he then do ?*

A. He went away into the forest near Uruvela, and spent six years in deep meditation, undergoing the severest discipline in mortifying his body.

52. Q. *Was he alone ?*

A. No ; five Brāhman companions attended him.

53. Q. *What were their names ?*

A. Kondañña, Bhaḍḍiya, Vappa, Mahānāma, and Assaji.

54. Q. *What plan of discipline did he adopt to open his mind to know the whole truth ?*

A. He sat and meditated, concentrating his mind upon, the higher problems of life, and shutting out from his sight and hearing all that was likely to interrupt his inward reflections.

55. Q. *Did he fast ?*

A. Yes, through the whole period. He took less and less food and water until, it is said, he ate scarcely more than one grain of rice or of sesamum seed each day.

56. Q. *Did this give him the wisdom he longed for* ?

A. No. He grew thinner and thinner in body and fainter in strength until, one day ,as he was slowly walking about and meditating, his vital force suddenly left him and he fell to the ground unconscious.

57. Q. *What did his companions think of that* ?

A. They fancied he was dead ; but after a time he revived.

58. Q. *What then* ?

A. The thought came to him that knowledge could never be reached by mere fasting or bodly suffering, but must be gained by the opening of the mind. He had just barely escaped death from self-starvation, yet had not obtained the Perfect Wisdom So he decided to eat, that he might live at least long enough to become wise.

59. Q. *Who gave him food* ?

A. He received food from Sujatā, a nobleman's daughter, who saw him sitting at the foot of a nyagroḍha (banyan) tree. He arose, took his alms-bowl, bathed in the river Nerañjarā, ate the food, and went into the jungle.

60. Q. *What did he do there* ?

A. Having formed his determination after these reflections, he went at evening to the Bōḍhi, or Asvaṭṭha tree, where the present Mahābōḍhi Temple stands.

61. Q. *What did he do there* ?

A. He determined not to leave the spot until he attained perfact wisdom.

62. Q. *At which side of the tree did he seat himself?*

A. The side facing the east.[1]

63. Q. *What did he obtain that night ?*

A. The knowledge of his previous births, of the causes of rebirths, and of the way to extinguish desires. Just before the break of the next day his mind was entirely opened, like the full—blown lotus flower ; the light of supreme knowledge, or the Four Truths, poured in upon him. He had become BUUḌḌHA —the Enlightened, the all-knowing—the *Sarvajña.*

64. Q. *Had he at last discovered the cause of human misery ?*

A. At last he had. As the light of the morning sun chases away the darkness of night, and reveals to sight the trees, fields, rocks, seas, rivers, animals, men and all things, so the full light of knowledge rose in his mind, and he saw at one glance the causes of human suffering and the way to escape from them.

65. Q. *Had he great struggles before gaining this perfect wisdom ?*

A. Yes, mighty and terrible struggles. He had to conquer in his body all those natural defects and human appetites and desires that prevent our seeing

[1]No reason is given in the canonical books for the choice of this side of the tree, though an explanation is to be found in the popular legends upon which the books of Bishop Bigandet and other European commentratos are based. There are always certain influences coming upon us from the different quarters of the sky. Sometimes the influence from one quarter will be best, sometimes that from another quarter. But the Buddha thought that the perfected man is superior to all extraneous influences.

the truth. He had to overcome all the bad influences of the sinful world around him. Like a soldier fighting desperately in battle against many enemies, he struggled : like a hero who conquers, he gained his object, and the secret of human misery was discovered.

66. Q. *What use did he make of the knowledge thus gained ?*

A. At first he was reluctant to teach it to the people at large.

67. Q. *Why ?*

A. Because of its profound importance and sublimity. He feared that but few people would understand it.

68. Q. *What made him alter this view ?*[1]

A. He saw that it was his duty to teach what he had learnt as clearly and simply as possible, and trust to the truth impressing itself upon the popular mind in proportion to each one's individual Karma. It was the only way of salvation, and every being had an equal right to have it pointed out to him. So he determined to begin with his five late companions, who had abandoned him when he broke his fast.

69. Q. *Where did he find them ?*

A. In the deer-park at Isipatana, near Benares.

70. Q. *Can he spot be now identified ?*

A. Yes, a partly ruined sṭūpa, or dagoba, is still standing on that very spot.

---

[1] The ancient story is that the God Brahmā himself implored him not to withhold the glorious truth.

71. Q. *Did those five companions readily listen to him ?*

A. At first, no ; but so great was the spiritual beauty of his appearance, so sweet and convincing his teaching, that they soon turned and gave him the closest attention.

72. Q. *What effect did this discourse have upon them ?*

A. The aged Kondañña, one who "understood" (*Aṅña*), was the first to lose his prejudices, accept the Buḍḍha's teaching, become his disciple, and enter the Path leading to Arhaṭship. The other four soon followed his example.

73. Q. *Who were his next converts ?*

A. A rich young layman, named Yasa, and his father, a wealthy merchant. By the end of three months the disciples numbered sixty persons.

74. Q. *Who were the first women lay disciples ?*

A. The mother and wife of Yasa.

75. Q. *What did the Buḍḍha do at that time ?*[1]

A. He called the disciples together, gave them full instructions, and sent them out in all directions to preach his doctrine.

76. Q. *What was the essence of it ?*

A. That the way of emancipation lies in leading the holy life and following the rules laid down, which will be explained later on.

---

[1] Brāhmanism not being offered to non-Hinḍūs, Buḍḍhism is consequently, the oldest missionary religion in the world. The early missionaries endured every hardship, cruelty, and persecution, with unfaltering courage.

77. Q. *Tell me what name he goes to this course of life ?*

A. The Noble Eightfold Path.

78. Q. *How is it called in the Pālī language ?*

A. *Ariyo atthangiko maggo.*

79. Q. *Whither did the Buḍḍha then go ?*

A. To Uruvela

80. Q. *What happened there ?*

A. He converted a man named Kāshyapa, renowned for his learning and teacher of the Jatilas, a great sect of fire-worshippers, all of whom became also his followers.

81. Q. *Who was his next great convert ?*

A. King Bimbisāra, of Magaḍha

82. Q. *Which two of the Buḍḍha's most learned and beloved disciples were converted at about this time ?*

A. Sāriputṛa and Moggallāna, formerly chief disciples of Sañjaya, the ascetic.

83. Q. *For what did they become renowned ?*

A. Sāriputṛa for his profound learning (*Prajña*), Moggallāna for his exceptional spiritual powers (*Iḍḍhi*).

84. Q. *Are these wonder-working powers miraculous ?*

A. No, but natural to all men and capable of being developed by a certain course of training.

85. Q. *Did the Buḍḍha hear again from his family after leaving them* ?

A. Oh yes, seven years later, while he was leving at Rājagṛha, his father King Suḍḍhoḍana, sent a message to request him to come and let him see him again before he died.

86. Q. *Did he go* ?

A. Yes. His father went with all his relations and ministers to meet him and received him with great joy.

87. Q. *Did he consent to resume his old rank* ?

A. No. In all sweetness he explained to his father that the Prince Siḍḍhārṭha had passed out of existence, as such, and was now changed into the condition of a Buḍḍha, to whom all beings were equally akin and equally dear. Instead of ruling over one tribe or nation, like an earthly king, he, through his Ḍharma, would win the hearts of all men to be his followers.

88. Q. *Did he see Yasoḍharā his son Rāhula* ?

A. Yes. His wife, who had mourned for him with deepest love, wept bitterly. She also sent Rāhula to ask him to give him his inheritance, as the son of a prince.

89. Q. *What happened* ?

A. To one and all he preached the Ḍharma as the cure for all sorrows. His father, son, wife, Ānanḍa (his half-brother), Ḍevaḍaṭṭa (his cousin and brother-in law), were all converted and became his disiciples. Two other famous ones were Anuruḍḍha, afterwards a great metaphysician, and Upāli, a barber, afterwards the greatest authority on *Vinaya*. Both of these gained great renown.

90. Q. *Who was the first Bhikkhum ?*

A. Prajāpaṭī, the aunt and foster-mother of Prince Siḍḍhārṭha. With her, Yasoḍharā and many other ladies were admitted into the Order as *Bhikkhunis* or female devotees.

91. Q. *What effect did the taking up of the religious life by his sons, Siḍḍharṭha and Ānanḍa, his nephew, Ḍevadaṭṭa, his son's wife, Yasoḍharā, and his grandson, Rāhula, have upon the old King Suḍḍhoḍana ?*

A. It grieved him much and he complained to the Buḍḍha, who then made it a rule of the Order that no person should thenceforth be ordained without the consent of his parents if alive.

92. Q. *Tell me about the fate of Ḍevaḍaṭṭa ?*

A. He was a man of great intelligence and ɪapidly advanced in the knowledge of the Ḍharma, but being also extremely ambitious, he came to envy and hate the Buḍḍha, and at last plotted to kill him. He also influenced Ajāṭashaṭru, son of King Bimbisāra, to murder his noble father, and to become his—Ḍevaḍaṭṭa's—disciple.

93. Q. *Did he do any injury to the Buḍḍha ?*

A. Not the least, but the evil he plotted against him recoiled upon himself, and he met with an awful death.

94. Q. *For how many years was the Buḍḍha engaged in teaching ?*

A. Forty-five years, during which time he preached a great many discourses. His custom and ṭhaṭ of his disciples was to travel and ṗreach during the eight dry months, but during the season of Wās—the rains—he and they would stop in the pansulas and vihārās which had been built for them by various kings and other wealthy converts.

95. Q. *Which were the most famous of these buildings ?*

A. Jetāvanārāma ; Veluvanārāma ; Pubbārāma ; Nigroḍhārāma and Isipatanārāma.

96. Q. *What kind of people were converted by him and his disciples ?*

A. People of all ranks, nations and castes ; rājas and coolies, rich and poor, mighty and humble, the illiterate and the most learned. His doctrine was suited to all.

97. Q. *Give some account of the decease of the Buḍḍha ?*

A. In the forty-fifth season after his attaining Buḍḍhahood, on the full-moon day of May, knowing that his end was near, he came at evening to Kusināgāra, a place about one hundred and twenty miles from Benares. In the sāla grove of the Mallas, the Upavarṭana of Kusinagara, between two sāla trees, he had his bedding spread with the head towards the north according to the ancient custom. He lay upon it, and with his mind perfectly clear, gave his final instructions to his disciples and bade them farewell.

98. Q. *Did he also make new converts in those last tours ?*

A. Yes, a very important one, a great Brāhmaṇa paṇḍiṭ named Subhaḍra. He had also preached to the Malla princes and their followers.

99. Q. *At day-break what happened ?*

A. He passed into the interior condition of *Samāḍhi* and thence into Nirvāṇa.

100. Q. *What were his last words to his disciples ?*

A. " Bhikkhus ", he said, " I now impress it upon you, the parts and powers of man must be dissolved. Work out your salvation with diligence ".

101. Q. *What convincing proof have we that the Buḍḍha, formerly Prince Siḍḍhārṭha, was a historical personage ?*

A. His existence is apparently as clearly proved as that of any other character of ancient history.

102. Q. *Name some of the proofs ?*

A. (1) The testimony of those who personally knew him.

(2) The discovery of places and the remains of buildings mentioned in the narrative of his time.

(3) The rock-inscriptions, pillars and dagobas made in memory of him by sovereigns who were near enough to his time to be able to verify the story of his life.

(4) The unbroken existence of the Saṅgha which he founded, and their possession of the facts of his life transmitted from generation to generation from the beginning.

(5) The fact that in the very year of his death and at various times subsequently, conventions and councils of the Saṅgha were held, for the verification of the actual teachings of the Founder, and the handing down of those verified teachings from teacher to pupil, to the present day.

(6) After his cremation his relics were divided among eight kings and a sṭūpa was erected over each portion. The portion given to King Ajātashaṭru, and by him covered with a sṭūpa at Rājagṛha, was taken, less that two centuries later, by the Emperor Asoka and distributes throughout his Empire. He of course, had ample means of knowing whether the relics were those of the Buḍḍha or not, since they had been in charge of the royal house of Patna from the beginning.

(7) Many of the Buḍḍha's disciples, being Arhaṭs and thus having control over their vital powers, must have lived to great ages, and there was nothing to have prevented two or three of them, in succession to each other, to have covered the whole period between the death of the Buddha and the reign of Asoka, and thus to have enabled the latter to get from his contemporary every desired attestation of the fact of the Buḍḍha's life.[1]

(8) The " Mahāvansa, " the best authenticated ancient history known to us, records the events of Sinhalese history to the reign of King Vijaya, 543 B.C. —almost the time of the Buḍḍha—and gives most

[1]At the Second Council there were two pupils of Ananda, consequently centenarians, while in Asoka's Council there were pupils of those pupils.

particulars of his life, as well as those of the Emperor Asoka and all other sovereigns related to Buḍḍhistic history.

103. Q. *By what names of respect is the Buḍḍha called ?*

A. Sākyamuni (the Sākya Sage) ; Sākya-Simha (the Sākyan Lion) ; Sugaṭa (the Happy One) ; Sattha (the Teacher) ; Jina (the Conqueror) ; Bhagavaṭ (the Blessed One) ; Lokanāṭha (the Lord of the World) ; Sarvajña (the Omniscient One) ; Ḍharmarāja (the King of Truth) ; Ṭaṭhāgaṭa (the Great Being), etc.

PART II

THE ḌHARMA OR DOCTRINE

106. Q. *What is the meaning of the word Buḍḍha?*

A. The enlightened, or he who has the perfect wisdom.

107. Q. *You have said that there were other Buḍḍhas before this one?*

A. Yes; our belief is that, under the operation of eternal causation, a Buḍḍha takes birth at intervals, when mankind have become plunged into misery through ignorance, and need the wisdom which it is the function of a Buḍḍha to teach. (See also Q. 11.)

108. Q. *How is a Buḍḍha developed?*

A. A person, hearing and seeing one of the Buḍḍhas on earth, becomes seized with the determination so to live that at some future time, when he shall become fitted for it, he also will be a Buḍḍha for the guiding of mankind out of the cycle of rebirth.

109. Q. *How does he proceed?*

A. Throughout that birth and every succeeding one, he strives to subdue his passions, to gain wisdom by experience, and to develop his higher faculties. He thus grows by degrees wiser, nobler in character, and stronger in virtue until, finally, after numberless re-births he reaches the state when he can become Perfected, Enlightened, All-wise, the ideal Teacher of the human race.

110. Q. *While this gradual development is going on throughout all these births, by what name do we call him ?*

A. Bōḍhisaṭ, or Bōḍhisaṭṭva. Thus the Prince Siḍḍhārtha Gauṭama was a Bōḍhisaṭṭva up to the moment when, under the blessed Bōḍhi tree at Gayā, he became Buḍḍha.

111. Q. *Have we any account of his various rebirths as a Bōḍhisaṭṭva ?*

A. In the *Jātakatthakathā*, a book containing stories of the Bōḍhisaṭṭva's reincarnations there are several hundred tales of that kind.

112. Q. *What lesson do these stories teach ?*

A. That a man can carry, throughout a long series of reincarnations, one great good purpose which enables him to conquer bad tendencies and develop virtuous ones.

113. Q. *Can we fix the number of reincarnations through which a Bōḍhisaṭṭva must pass before he can become a Buḍḍha ;*

A. Of course not : that depends upon his natural character, the state of development to which he has arrived when he forms the resolution to become a Buḍḍha, and other things.

114. Q. *Have we a way of classifying Bōḍhisaṭṭvas ? If so, explain it.*

A. Bōḍhisaṭṭvas—the future Buḍḍhas—are divided into three classes.

115. Q. *Proceed. How are these three kinds of Bōḍhisaṭs named ?*

A. Pannāḍhika, or Uḍghatitajña—"he who attains least quickly "; Saḍḍhāḍhika, or Vipachitajña

—"he who attains less quickly "; and Vīryāḍhika, or Gneyya—"he who attains quickly". The Pannāḍhika Bōḍhisaṭs take the course of Intelligence ; the Saḍḍhaḍhika take the course of Faith ; the Viryāḍhika take the course of energetic Action. The first is guided by Intelligence and does not hasten ; the second is full of Faith, and does not care to take the guidance of Wisdom ; and the third never delays to do what is good. Regardless of the consequence to himself, he does it when he sees that it is best that it should be done.

116. Q. *When our Bōḍhisaṭṭva became Buḍḍha, what did he see was the cause of human misery ? Tell me in one word.*

A. Ignorance (*Aviḍyā*).

117. Q. *Can you tell me the remedy ?*

A. To dispel Ignorance and become wise (*Prājña*).

118. Q. *Why does ignorance cause suffering ?*

A. Because it makes us prize what is not worth prizing, grieve when we should not grieve, consider real what is not real but only illusionary, and pass our lives in the pursuit of worthless objects, neglecting what is in reality most valuable.

119. Q. *And what is that which is most valuable ?*

A. To know the whole secret of man's existence and destiny, so that we may estimate at no more than their actual value this life and its relations ; and so that we may live in a way to ensure the greatest happiness and the least suffering for our fellow-men and ourselves.

120. Q. *What is the light that can dispel this ignorance of ours and and remowe all sorrows* ?

A. The knowledge of the "Four Noble Truths," as the Buḍḍha called them.

121. Q. *Name these Four Noble Truths* ?

A. 1. The miseries of evolutionary existence resulting in births and deaths, life after life.

2. The cause productive of misery, which is the selfish desire, ever renewed, of satisfying on self, without being able ever to secure that end.

3. The destruction of that desire, or the estranging of one's self from it.

4. The means of obtaining this destruction of desire.

122. Q. *Tell me some things that cause sorrow* ?

A. Birth, decay, illness, death, separation from objects we love, association with those who are repugnant, craving for what cannot be obtained.

123. Q. *Do these differ with each individual* ?

A. Yes : but all men suffer from them in degree.

124. Q. *How can we escape the sufferings which result from unsatisfied desires and ignorant cravings* ?

A. By complete conquest over, and destruction of, this eager thirst for life and its pleasures, which causes sorrow.

125. Q. *How may we gain such a conquest* ?

A. By following the Noble Eight-fold Path which the Buḍḍha discovered and pointed out.

125. Q. *what do you mean by that word : what is this Noble Eight-fold Path* ? (For the Pāli name see Q. 79).

A. The eight parts of this path are called *aṅgas*. They are : 1. Right Belief (as to the law of Causation, or Karma) ; 2. Right Thought ; 3. Right Speech ; 4. Right Action ; 5. Right Means of Livelihood ; 6. Right Exertion ; 7. Right Remembrance and Self-discipline ; 8. Right Concentration of Thought. The man who keeps these *aṅgas* in mind and follows them will be free from sorrow and ultimately reach salvation.

127. Q. *Can you give a better word for salvation*?

A. Yes, emancipation.

128. Q. *Emancipation, then from what* ?

A. Emancipation from the miseries of earthly existence and of rebirths, all of which are due to ignorance and impure lusts and cravings.

129. Q. *And when this salvation or emancipation is attained, what do we reach* ?

A. NIRVANA.

130. Q. *What is Nirvāṇa* ?

A. A condition of total cessation of changes, of perfect rest, of the absence of desire and illusion and sorrow, of the total obliteration of everything that goes to make up the physical man. Before reaching Nirvāṇa man is constantly being reborn ; when he reaches Nirvāṇa he is born no more.

131. Q. *Where can be found a learned discussion of the word Nirvāṇa and a list of the other names by which the old Pālī writers attempt to define it ?*

A. In the famous *Dictionary of the Pālī Language*, by the late Mr. R. C. Childers, is a complete list.[1]

132. Q. *But some people imagine that Nirvāṇa is some sort of heavenly place, a Paradise. Does Buḍḍhism teach that ?*

A. No. When Kūtaḍanta asked the Buḍḍha "Where is Nirvāña," he replied that it was "wherever the precepts are obeyed "

133. Q. *What causes us to be reborn ?*

A. The unsatisfied selfish desire (Skt., *tṛshṇā* ; *Pālī, ṭanhā*) for things that belong to the state of personal existence in the material world. This unquenched thirst for physical existence (*bhāva*) is a force, and has a creative power in itself so strong that it draws the being back into mundane life.

134. Q. *Are our rebirths in any way affected by the nature of our unsatisfied desires ?*

A. Yes ; and by our individual merits or demerits.

135. Q. *Does our merit or demerit control the state, condition or form in which we shall be re-born ?*

A. It does. The broad rule is that if we have an excess of merit we shall be well and happily

[1]Mr. Childers takes a highly pessimistic view of the Nirvāṇic state, regarding it as annihilation. Later students disagree with him.

born the next time ; if an excess of demerit, our next birth will be wretched and full of suffering.

136. Q. *One chief pillar of Buḍḍhistic doctrine is, then, the idea that every effect is the result of an actual cause, is it not ?*

A. It is ; of a cause either immediate or remote.

137. Q. *What do we call this causation ?*

A. Applied to individuals, it is Karma, that is, action. It means that our own actions or deeds bring upon us whatever of joy or misery we experience.

138. Q. *Can a bad man escape from the outworkings of his Karma ?*

A. The *Ḍhammapaḍa* says : "There exist, no spot on the earth, or in the sky, or in the sea, neither is there any in the mountain-clefts, where an (evil) deed does not bring trouble (to the doer)."

139. Q. *Can a good man escape ?*

A. As the result of deeds of peculiar merit, a man may attain certain advantages of place, body, environment and teaching in his next stage of progress, which ward off the effects of bad Karma and help his higher evolution.

140. *What are they called ?*

A. *Gaṭi Sampaṭṭi, Upāḍhi Sampaṭṭi, Kala Sampaṭṭi and Payoga Sampaṭṭi.*

141. Q. *Is that consistent or inconsistent with common sense and the teachings of modern science ?*

A. Perfectly consistent : there can be no doubt of it.

142. Q. *May all men become Buḍḍhas ?*

A. It is not in the nature of every man to become a Buḍḍha ; for a Buḍḍha is developed only at long intervals of time, and seemingly, when the state of humanity absolutely requires such a teacher to show it the forgotten Path to Nirvāṇa. But every being may equally reach Nirvāṇa, by conquering Ignorance and gaining Wisdom.

143. Q. *Does Buḍḍhism teach that man is reborn only upon our earth ?*

A. As a general rule that would be the case, until he had evolved beyond its level ; but the inhabited worlds are numberless. The world upon which a person is to have his next birth, as well as the nature of the rebirth itself, is decided by the preponderance of the individual's merit or demerit. In other words, it will be controlled by his attractions, as science would describe it ; or by his Karma, as we, Buḍḍhists, would say.

144. Q. *Are there worlds more perfectly developed, and others less so than our Earth ?*

A. Buḍḍhism teaches that there are whole *Sakwalas*, or systems of worlds, of various kinds, higher and lower, and also that the inhabitants of each world correspond in development with itself.

145. Q. *Has not the Buḍḍha summed up his whole doctrine in one gāthā, or verse ?*

A. Yes.

145. Q. *Repeat it ?*

A. *Sabba pāpassa akaraṇam,*
Kusalassa upasampada
Sachiṭṭa pariyoḍapanam—
Eṭam Buḍḍhānusāsanam.

" To cease from all evil actions,
To generate all that is good,
To cleanse one's mind :
This is the constant advice of the Buḍḍhas ".

147. Q. *Have the first three of these lines any very striking characteristics ?*

A. Yes : the first line embodies the whole spirit of the *Vinaya Pitaka*, the second that of the *Suṭṭa*, the third that of the *Abhiḍhamma*. They comprise only eight Pālī words, yet, as the dew-drop reflects the stars, they sparkle with the spirit of all the Buḍḍha Ḍharma.

148. Q. *Do these precepts show that Buḍḍhism is an active or a passive religion ?*

A. To " cease from sin " may be called passive, but to " get virtue " and " to cleanse one's own heart ", or mind, are altogether *active* qualities. Buḍḍha taught that we should not merely not be evil, but that we should be *positively* good.

149. Q. *Who or what are the "Three Guides"*[1] *that a Buḍḍhist is supposed to follow* ?

A. They are disclosed in the formula called the Tisaraṇa : "I follow Buḍḍha as my Guide : I follow the Law as my Guide : I follow the Order as my Guide ". These three are, in fact, the Buḍḍha Ḍharma.

150. Q. *What does he mean when repeating this formula.*?

A. He means that he regards the Buḍḍha as his all-wise Teacher, Friend and Exemplar ; the law, or Doctrine, ascontaining the essential and immutable principles of Justice and Truth and the path that leads

---

[1]*Saraṇam.* Wijesinha Muḍaliar writes me : "This word has been hitherto very inappropriately and erroneously rendered *Refuge*, by European Pālī scholars, and thoughtlessly so accepted by native Pālī scholars. Neither Pālī etymology nor Buḍḍhistic philosophy justifies the translation. *Refuge*, in the sense of a *fleeing back or a place of shelter*, is quite foreign to true Buḍḍhism, which insists on every man working out his own emancipation. The root *Sṛ* in Samskrt (*sara* in Palī) means to move, to go ; so that *Saraṇam* would denote a moving, or he or that which goes before or with another—a Guide or helper. I construe the passage thus : *Gachchāmi*, I go, *Buḍḍham*, to Buḍḍha *Saraṇam*, as my Guide. The translation of the *Tisaruna* as the "Three Refuges," has given rise to much misapprehension, and has been made by anti-Buḍḍhists a fertile pretent for taunting Buḍḍhists with the absurdity of taking refuge in non-entities and believing in unrealities. The term refuge is more applicable to Nirvāṇa, of which *Saranam* is a synonym. The High Priest Sumaṇgala also calls my attention to the fact that the Pālī root *Sara* has the secondary meaning of killing, or that which destroys. *Buḍḍham saraṇam gachchhāmi* might thus be rendered "I go to Buḍḍha, the Law, and the Order, as the destroyers of my fears—the first by his preaching, the second by its axiomatic truth, the third by their various examples and precepts.".

to the realisation of perfect peace of mind on earth ; and the Order as the teachers and exemplars of that excellent Law taught by Buḍḍha.

151. Q. *But are not some of the members of this "Order" men intellectually and morally inferior ?*

A. Yes ; but we are taught by the Buḍḍha that only those who diligently attend to the Precepts, discipline their minds, and strive to attain or have attained one of the eight stages of holiness and perfection, constitute his "Order". It is expressly stated that the Order referred to in the "Tisaraṇa" refers to the "Attha Ariya Puggala"—the Noble Ones who have attained one of the eight stages of perfection. The mere wearing of yellow robes, or even ordination, does *not* of itself make a man pure or wise or entitle him to reverence.

152. Q. *Then it is not such unworthy bhikkhus as they, whom the true Buḍḍhist would take as his guides ?*

A. Certainly not.

153. Q. *What are the five observances, or universal precepts, called the Pañcha Sīla, which are imposed on the laity in general ?*

A. They are included in the following formula, which Buḍḍhists repeat publicly at the vihāras (temples) :

I observe the precept to refrain from destroying the life of beings.

I observe the precept to refrain from stealing.

I observe the precept to abstain from unlawful sexual intercourse.[1]

I observe the precept to refrain from falsehood.

I observe the precept to abstain from using intoxicants.

154. Q. *What strikes the intelligent person on reading these Sīlas ?*

A. That one who observes them strictly must escape from every cause productive of human misery. If we study history we shall find that it has all sprung from one or another of these causes.

155. Q. *In which Sīlas is the far-seeing wisdom of the Buḍḍha most plainly shown ?*

A. In the first, third and fifth ; for the taking of life, sensuality, and the use of intoxicants, cause at least ninety-five per cent of the sufferings among men.

156. Q. *What benefits does a man derive from the observance of these Precepts ?*

A. He is said to acquire more or less merit according to the manner and time of observing the precepts, and the number observed ; that is, if he observes only one precept, violating the other four, he acquires the merit of the observance of that precept only ; and the longer he keeps that precept the greater

---

1 This qualified form refers, of course, to laymen who only profess to keep five precepts : a Bhikkhu must observe strict celibacy. So, also, must the laity who binds himself to observe eight of the whole ten Precepts for specified periods ; during these periods he must be celibate. The five Precepts were laid down by Buḍḍha for all people. Though one may not be a Buḍḍhist, yet the five and eight Precepts may profitably be observed by all. It is the taking of the " Three Refuges " that constitutes one a Buddhist.

will be the merit. He who keeps all the precepts inviolate will cause himself to have a higher and happier existence hereafter.

157. Q. *What are the other observances which it is considered meritorious for the laity as such to undertake voluntarily to keep ?*

A. The *Aṭṭhaṅga Sīla,* or the Eightfold Precept, which embraces the five above enumerated (omitting the work " unlawful " in the third), with three additional ; *viz :*

I observe the precept to abstain from eating at an unseasonable time.

I observe the precept to abstain from dancing, singing, music and unbecoming shows, and from the use of garlands, scents, perfumes, cosmetics, ointments, and ornaments.

I observe the precept to abstain from using high and broad beds.

The seats and couches here referred to are those used by the worldly-minded for the sake of pleasure and sensual enjoyment. The celibate should avoid these.

158. Q. *How would a Buḍḍhist describe true merit ?*

A. There is no great merit in any merely outward act ; all depends upon the inward motive that provokes the deed.

159. Q. *Give an example ?*

A. A rich man may expend lakhs of rupees in building dāgobās or vihāras, in erecting statues of Buḍḍha, in festivals and processions, in feeding priests, in giving alms to the poor, or in planting trees, digging tanks, or constructing rest-houses by the roadside for travellers, and yet have comparatively little merit if it be done for display, or to hear himself praised by men, or for any other selfish motives. But he who does the least of these things with a kind motive, such as love for his fellow-men, gains great merit. A good deed done with a bad motive benefits others, but not the doer. One who approves of a good deed when done by another shares in the merit, *if his sympathy is real, not pretended.* The same rule applies to evil deeds.

160. Q. *But which is said to be the greatest of all meritorious actions ?*

A. The *Dhammapada* declares that the merit of disseminating the Ḍharma, the Law of Righteousness, is greater than that of any other good work.

161. Q. *What books contain all the most excellent wisdom of the Buḍḍha's teachings ?*

A. The three collections of books called *Ţripitakas* or " *Three Baskets* ".

162. Q. *What are the names of the three Pitakas, or groups of books ?*

A. The *The Vinaya Pitaka,* the *Suṭṭa Pitaka* and the *Abhiḍhamma Pitaka.*

163. Q. *What do they respectively contain ?*

A. The first contains all that pertains to morality and the rules of discipline for the government of the Saṅgha, or Order ; the second contains instructive discourses on ethics applicable to all ; the third explains the psychological teachings of the Buḍḍha including the twenty-four transcendental laws explanatory of the workings of Nature.

164. Q. *Do Buḍḍhists believe these books to be inspired, or revealed by a Divine Being ?*

A. No ; but they revere them as containing all the parts of that most Excellent Law, by the knowing of which man may break through the trammels of *Samsāra.*

165. Q. *In the whole text of the three Pitakas how many words are there ?*

A. Dr. Rhys-Davids estimates them at 1,752,800.

165. Q. *When were the Pitakas first reduced to writing ?*

A. In 88-76 B.C., under the Sinhalese King, Wattagamini, or three hundred and thirty years after the Paranāvirana of the Buḍḍha.

167. Q. *Have we reason to believe that all the discourses of the Buḍḍha are known to us ?*

A. Probably not, and it would be strange if they were. Within the forty-five years of his public life he must have preached many hundreds of discourses. Of these, in times of war and persecution, many must have been lost, many scattered to distant countries, and many mutilated, History says that enemies of the Buḍḍha Ḍhamma burnt piles of our books as high as a coco-nut tree.

168. Q. *Do Buddhists consider the Buddha as one who by his own virtue can save us from the consequence of our individual sins ?*

A. Not at all. Man must emancipate himself. Until he does that he will continue being born over and over and over again—the victim of ignorance, the slave of unquenched passions.

169. Q. *What, then, was the Buddha to us, and all other beings ?*

A. An all-seeing, all-wise Counsellor ; one who discovered the safe path and pointed it out ; one who showed the cause of, and the only cure for, human suffereing. In pointing to the road, in showing us how to escape dangers, he became our Guide. He is to us like one leading blind man across a narrow bridge over a swift and deep stream and so saving his life.

170. Q. *If we were to try to represent the whole spirit of the Buddha's doctrine by one word, which word should we choose ?*

A. Justice.

171. Q. *Why ?*

A. Because it teaches that every man gets, under the operations of unerring KARMA, exactly that reward or punishment which he has deserved, no more and no less. No good deed or bad deed, however trifling, and however secretly committed, escapes the evenly-balanced scales of Karma.

172. Q. *What is Karma* ?[1]

A. A causation operating on the moral, as well as on the physical and other planes. Buḍḍhists say there is no miracle in human affairs : what a man sows that he must and will reap.

173. Q. *What other good words have been used to express the essence of Buḍḍhism* ?

A. Self-culture and universal love.

174. Q. *What doctrine ennobles Buddhism, and gives it its exalted place among the world's religions* ?

A. That of *Miṭṭa* or *Maiṭreya*—compassionate kindness. The importance of this doctrine is moreover emphasised in the giving of the name " Maiṭri " (the Compassionate One), to the coming Buddha.

175. Q. *Were all these points of Doctrine that yoy have explained meditated upon by the Buḍḍha near the Bo-tree* ?

A. Yes, these and many more that may be read in the Buḍḍhist Scriptures. The entire system of Buḍḍhism came to his mind during the Great Enlightenment.

175. *How long did the Buḍḍha remain near the Bo tree* ?

A. Forty-nine days.

---

[1] Karma is defined as the sum total of a man's actions. The law of Cause and Effect is called the *Paticcla Samuppada Dhamma*. In the *Anguṭṭara Nikaya* the Buḍḍha teaches that my action is my possession, my action is my inheritance, my action is the womb which bears me, my action is my relative, my action is my refuge.

177. Q. *What do we call the first discourse preached by the Buḍḍha—that which he addressed to his five former companions ?*

A. The *Ḍhammacakka-ppavaṭṭana suṭṭa*—the Suṭra of the Definition of the Rules of Doctrine.[1]

178. Q. *What subjects were treated by him in this discourse ?*

A. The "Four Noble Truths," and the "Noble Eightfold Path". He condemned the extreme physical mortification of the ascetics, on the one hand, and the enjoyment of sensual pleasures on the other ; pointing out and recommending the Noble Eightfold Path as the Middle Path.

179. Q. *Did the Buḍḍha hold with idol-worship ?*

A. He did not ; he opposed it. The worship of gods, demons, trees, etc., was condemned by the Buḍḍha. External worship is a fetter that one has to break if he is to advance higher.

---

[1]After the appearance of the first edition, I received from one of the ablest Pali scholars of Ceylon, the late L. Corneille Wijesinha Esq., Mudaliar of Matale, what seems a better rendering of, *Dhammacakka-pparaṭṭana* than the one previously given ; he makes it "The Establishment of the Reign of Law". Professor Rhys-Davids prefers, "The Foundation of the Kingdom of Righteousness. Mr. Wijesingha writes me : "You may use 'Kingdom of Righteousness,' too, but it savours more of dogmatic theology than philosophic ethics. *Dhammacakkappavaṭṭama suṭṭam* is the discourse entitled 'The Establishment of the Reign of Law'." Having shown this to the High Priest, I am happy to be able to say that he assents to Mr. Wijesingha's rendering.

180. *Q. But do not Buḍḍhists make revence before the statue of the Buḍḍha, his relics, and the monuments enshrining him ?*

A. Yes, but not with the sentiment of the idolater.

181. Q. *What is the difference ?*

A. Our Pagan brother not only takes his images as visible representations of his unseen God or gods, but the refined idolater, in worshipping, considers that the idol contains in its substance a portion of the all-pervading divinity.

182. Q. *What does the Buḍḍhist think ?*

A. The Buḍḍhist reverences the Buḍḍha's statue and the other things you have mentioned, only as momentoes of the greatest, wisest, most benevolent and compassionate man in this world-period (Kalpa). All races and people preserve, treasure up, and value the relics and momentoes of men and women who have been considered in any way great. The Buḍḍha, to us, seems more to be revered and beloved than any one else, by every human being who knows sorrow.

183. Q. *Has the Buḍḍha himself given us something definite upon this subject ?*

A. Certainly. In the *Mahā Pari-Nirvāna Suṭṭa* he says that emancipation is attainable only by leading the Holy life, according to the Noble Eightfold Path, not by eternal worship (*āmisa pūjā*), nor by adoration of himself, or of another, or of any image.

184. Q. *What was the Buḍḍha's estimate of ceremonialism?*

A. From the beginning, he condemned the observance of ceremonies and other external practices, which only tend to increase our spiritual blindness and our clinging to mere lifeless forms.

185. Q. *What as to controversies?*

A. In numerous discourses he denounced this habit as most pernicious. He prescribed penances for Bhikkhus who waste time and weaken their higher intuitions in wrangling over theories and metaphysical subtleties.

185. A. *Are charms, incantations, the observance of lucky hours and devil-dancing a part of Buḍḍhism?*

A. They are positively repugnant to its fundamental principles. They are the surviving relics of fetishism and pantheism and other foreign religions. In the *Brāhmajāla Suṭṭa* the Buḍḍha has categorically described these and other superstitions as Pagan, mean and spurious.[1]

187. Q. *What striking contrasts are there between Buḍḍhism and what may be properly called "religions"?*

A. Among others, these: It teaches the highest goodness without a creating God; a continuity of line without adhering to the superstitious and selfish

[1]The mixing of these arts and practices with Buḍḍhism is a sign of deterioration. Their facts and phenomena are real and capable of scientific explanation. They are embraced in the term "magic," but when resorted to, for selfish purposes, attract bad influences about one, and impede spiritual advancement. When employed for harmless and beneficent purposes, such as healing the sick, saving life, etc., the Buḍḍha permitted their use.

doctrine of an eternal, metaphysical soul-substance that goes out of the body; a hapiness without an objective heaven; a method of salvation without a vicarious Saviour; redemtpion by oneself as the Redeemer, and without rites, prayers, penances, priest or intercessory saints; and a *summum bonum*, *i.e.*, Nirvāna, attainable in this life and in this world by leading a pure, unselfish life of wisdom and of compassion to all beings.

188. Q. *Specify the two main divisions of "meditation," i.e., of the process by which one extinguishes passion and attains knowledge* ?

A. *Samatha* and *Viḍarsana* : (1) the attenuation of passion by leading the holy life and by continued effort to subdue the senses ; (2) the attainment of supernormal wisdom by reflection : each of which embraces twenty aspects, but I need not here specify them.

189. Q. *What are the four paths or stages of advancement that one may attain to* ?

A. (1) *Sotāpatti*—the beginning or entering into which follows after one's clear perception of the "Four Noble Truths" ; (2) *Sakarḍāgāmi*—the path of one who has so subjugated lust, hatred and delusion that he need only return once to this world ; (3) *Anāgami*—the path of those who have so far conquered self that they need not return to this world ; (4) *Arhaṭ*—the path of the holy and worthy Arhaṭ, who is not only free from the necessity of reincarnation, but has capacitated himself to enjoy perfect wisdom, boundless pity for the ignorant and suffering, and measureless love for all beings.

190. Q. *Does popular Buḍḍhism contain nothing but what is true, and in accord with science ?*

A. Like every other religion that has existed many centuries, it certainly now contains untruth mingled with truth ; even gold is found mixed with dross. The poetical imagination, the zeal, or the lingering superstition of Buḍḍhist devotees have, in various ages, and in various lands, caused the noble principles of the Buḍḍha's moral doctrines to be coupled more or less with what might be removed to advantage.

191. Q. *When such perversions are discovered, what should be the true Buḍḍhist's earnest desire ?*

A. The true Buddhist should be ever ready and anxious to see the false purged away from the true, and to assist, if he can. Three great Councils of the Saṅgha were held for the express purpose of purging the body of Teachings from all corrupt interpolations.

192. Q. *When ?*

A. The first, at Sattapanni cave, just after the death of the Buḍḍha ; the second at Valukarama, in Vaisāli ; the third at Asokarama Vihāra, at Pātaliputra, 235 years after Buḍḍha's decease.

193. Q. *In what discourse does the Buḍḍha himself warn us to expect this perversion of the true Doctrine ?*

A. In the *Sanyuṭṭa Nikāya.*

194. Q. *Are there any dogmas in Buḍḍhism which we are required to accept on faith ?*

A. No: we are earnestly enjoined to accept nothing whatever on faith ; whether it be written in books, handed down from our ancestors, or taught by the sages.

195. Q. *Did he himself really teach that noble rule ?*

A. Yes. The Buḍḍha has said that we must not believe in a thing said merely because it is said ; nor in traditions because they have been handed down from antiquity ; nor rumours, as such ; nor writings by sages, merely because sages wrote them ; nor fancies that we may suspect to have been inspired in us by a Ḍeva (that is, in presumed spiritual inspiraition) ; nor from inferences drawn from some haphazard assumption we may have made ; nor because of what seems analogical necessity ; nor on the mere authority of our own teachers or masters.

196. Q. *When, then, must we believe?*

A. We are to believe when the writing doctrine or saying is corroborated by our own reason and consciousness. " For this, " says he in concluding " I taught you not to believe merely because you have heard, but when you believed of your own consciousness, then to act accordingly and abundantly." (See the *Kālāma Suṭṭa* of the *Anguṭṭara Nikāya*, and the *Mahā Pari Nirvāna Suṭṭa.*)

197. Q. *What does the Buḍḍha call himself ?*

A. He says that he and the other Buḍḍhas are only " preachers " of truth who point out the way : we ourselves must make the effort.

198. Q. *Where is this said ?*

A. In the *Ḍhammapaḍa.*, Chapter xx.

199. Q. *Does Buḍḍhism countenance hypocrisy* ?

A. The *Ḍhammapaḍa says :* "Like a beautiful flower full of colour without scent the fine words of him who does not act accordingly are fruitless."

200. Q. *Does Buḍḍhism teach us to return evil for evil* ?

A. In the *Ḍhammapaḍa* the Buḍḍha said : "If a man foolishly does me wrong, I will return to him the protection of my ungrudging love ; the more evil comes from him, the more good shall go from me." This is the path followed by the Arhaṭ.[1] To return evil for evil is positively forbidden in Buḍḍhism.

---

[1] A Buḍḍhist ascetic who, by a prescribed course of practice, has attained to a superior state of spiritual and intellectual development. Arhaṭs may be divided into the two general groups of the *Samathayanika* and *Sukka Vipassaka.* The former have destroyed their passions, and fully developed their intellectual capacity or mystical insight ; the latter have equally conquered passion, but not acquired the superior mental powers. The former can work phenomena, the latter cannot. The Arhaṭ of the former class, when fully developed, is no longer a prey to the delusions of the senses, nor the slave of passion or mortal frailty. *He penetrates to the root of whatsoever subject his mind is applied to* without following the slow processes of reasoning. His self-conquest is complete ; and in place of the emotion and desire which vex and enthral the ordinary man, he is lifted up into a condition which is best expressed in the term "Nirvāṇic". There is in Ceylon a popular misconception that the attainment of Arhaṭship is now impossible ; that the Buḍḍha had himself prophesied that the power would die out in one millenium after his death. This rumour—and the similar one that is everywhere heard in India, *viz.*, that this being the dark cycle of the *Kali Yuga*, the practice of Yoga Viḍyā, or sublime spiritual science, is impossible—I ascribe to the ingenuity of those who should be as pure and (to use a non-Buḍḍhistic but very convenient term) *psychically* wise as were their predecessors, but are not, and

201. Q. *Does it encourage cruelty* ?

A. No, indeed. In the Five Precepts and in many of his discourses, the Buḍḍha teaches us to be merciful to all beings, to try and make them happy, to love them all, to abstain from taking life, or consenting to it, or encouraging its being done.

202. Q. *In which discourse is this stated* ?

A. The *Ḍhammika Suṭṭa* says : "Let him (the householder) not destroy, or cause to be destroyed, any life at all, or *sanction the act of those who do so*. Let him refrain from even hurting any creature."[1]

203. Q. *Does it approve of drunkenness* ?

A. In his *Ḍhammika Suṭṭa* we are warned against drinking liquors, causing others to drink, or sanctioning the acts of those who drink.[2]

204. Q. *To what are we told that drunkeness leads* ?

A. To demerit, crime, insanity, and ignorance —which is the chief cause of rebirth.

---

who therefore seek an excuse ! The Buḍḍha taught quite the contrary idea. In the *niga dikāya* he said : "Hear, Subbhaḍra ! The world will never be without Arhaṭs if the ascetics (Bhikkhus) in my congregations *well and truly keep my precepts*." (*Imeccha Subhaddabhikku samma vihareyyum asunno loko Arahantehiassa*).

[1] Kolb, in his *History of Culture*, says : "It is Buḍḍhism we have to thank for the sparing of prisoners of war, who heretofore had been slain ; also for the discontinuance of the carrying away into captivity of the inhabitants of conquered lands.

[2] The fifth Sila has reference to the mere taking of intoxicants and stupefying drugs, which leads ultimately to drunkenness.

205. Q. *What does Buḍḍhism teach about marriage* ?

A. Absolute chastity being a condition of full spiritual development, is most highly commended ; but a marriage to one wife and fidelity to her is recognised as a kind of chastity. Polygamy was censured by the Buḍḍha as involving ignorance and promoting lust.

206. Q.. *In what discourse* ?

A. The *Anguṭṭara Nikāya*, Chapter iv, 55.

207. Q. *What does it teach as to the duty of parents to children* ?

A. They should restrain them from vice ; train them in virtue ; have them taught arts and sciences ; provide them with suitable wives and husbands, and give them their inheritance.

208. Q. *What is the duty of children* ?

A. To support their parents when old or needy ; perform family duties incumbent on them ; guard their property ; make themselves worthy to be their heirs, and when they are gone, honour their memory.

209. Q. *What of pupils to the teacher* ?

A. To show him respect ; minister to him ; obey him ; supply his wants ; attend to his instruction.

210. Q. *What of husband to wife* ?

A. To cherish her ; treat her with respect and kindness ; be faithful to her ; cause her to be honoured by others ; provide her with suitable ornaments and clothes.

211. Q. *What of the wife to her husband ?*

A. To show affection to him ; order her household aright ; be hospitable to guests ; be chaste ; be thrifty ; show skill and diligence in all things.

212. Q. *Where are these precepts taught ?*

A. In the *Sigālovāda Suṭṭa.*

213. Q. *Do riches help a man to future happiness ?*

A. The *Ḍhammapaḍa* says : "One is the road that leads to wealth, another the road that leads to Nirvāṇa."

214. Q. *Does that mean that no rich man can attain Nirvāṇa ?*

A. That depends on which he loves most. If he uses his wealth for the benefit of mankind—for the suffering, the oppressed, the ignorant—then his wealth aids him to acquire merit.

215. Q. *But if the contrary ?*

A. But if he loves and greedily hoades money for the sake of its possession, then it weakens his moral sense, prompts him to crime, brings curses upon him in this life, and their effects are felt in the next birth.

215. Q. *What says the "Ḍhammapaḍa" about ignorance ?*

A. That it is a taint worse than all taints that a man can put upon himself.

217. Q. *What does it say about uncharitableness towards others ?*

A. That the fault of others is easily perceived but that of oneself difficult to perceive ; a man winnows his neighbour's faults like chaff, but his own fault he hides, as a cheat hides the bad die from the gambler.

218. Q. *What advice does the Buḍḍha give us as to man's duty to the poor* ?

A. He says that a man's net income should be divided into four parts, of which one should be devoted to philanthropic objects.

219. Q. *What five occupations are said to be low and base* ?

A. Selling liquor, selling animals for slaughter, selling poison, selling murderous weapons, and dealing in slaves.

220. Q. *Who are said to be incapable of progress in spirituality* ?

A. The killers of father, mother, and holy Arhaṭs; Bhikkhus who sow discord in the Sangha ; those who attempt to injure the person of a Buḍḍha; those who hold extremely nihilistic views as to the future existence ; and those who are extremely sensual.

121. Q. *Does Buḍḍhism specify places or conditions of torment into which a bad man's Karma draws him on leaving this life* ?

A. Yes. They are : Sanjīva ; Kālasuṭra ; Saṅghāṭa ; Raurava ; Mahā-Raurava Ṭāpa ; Praṭāpa ; Avīchi.

222. Q. *Is the torment eternal* ?

A. Certainly not. Its duration depends on a man's Karma.

223. Q. *Does Buḍḍhism declare that non-believers in Buḍḍha will of necessity be damned for their unbelief* ?

A. No ; by good deeds they may enjoy a limited term of happiness before being drawn into rebirth by their unexhausted *ṭanhā*. To escape rebirth, one *must* tread the Noble Eight-fold Path.

224. Q. *What is the spiritual status of woman among Buḍḍhist* ?

A. According to our religion they are on a footing of perfect equality with men. " Woman," says the Buḍḍha, in the *Chullavedalla Suṭṭa*, " may attain the highest path of holiness that is open to man—Arhaṭship."

225. Q. *What does a modern critic say about the effect of Buḍḍhism on woman* ?

A. That " it has done more for the happiness and enfranchisement of woman than any other creed " (Sir Lepel Griffin).

226. Q. *What did the Buḍḍha teach about caste* ?

A. That one does not become of any caste, whether Pariah, the lowest, or Brāhmaṇa the highest, by birth, but by deeds. " By deeds," said He, " one becomes an outcast, by deeds one becomes a Brāhmaṇa " (See *Vasala Suṭṭa*).

227. Q. *Tell me a story to illustrate this* ?

A. Ānanḍa, passing by a well, was thirsty and asked Prakṛṭti, a girl of the Māṭanga, or Pariah, caste, to give him water. She said she was of such low caste that he would become contaminated by taking water from her hand. But Ānanḍa replied : " I ask not for caste but for water " ; and the Māṭanga girl's heart was glad and she gave him to drink. The Buḍḍha blessed her for it.

228. Q. *What did the Buḍḍha say in " Vasala Suṭṭa " about a man of the Pariah Sopāka caste* ?

A. That by his merits he reached the highest fame ; that many Khaṭṭiyas (Kṣhaṭṭriyas) and Brāhmaṇas went to serve him ; and that after death he was born in the Brahmā-world : while there are many Brāhmaṇas who for their evil deeds are born in hell.

229. Q. *Does Buḍḍhism teach the immortality of the soul ?*

A. It considers " soul " to be a word used by the ignorant to express a false idea. If everything is subject to change, then man is included, and every material part of him must change. That which is subject to change is not permanent : so there can be no immortal survival of a changeful thing.[1]

230. Q. *What is so objectionable in this word " soul " ?*

A. The idea associated with it that man can be an entity separated from all other entities, and from the existence of the whole of the Universe. This idea of separateness is unreasonable, not provable by logic, nor supported by science.

231. Q. *Then there is no separate "I", nor can we say " my " this or that ?*

A. Exactly so.

232. Q. *If the idea of a separate human "soul" is to be rejected, what is it in man which gives him the impression of having a permanent personality ?*

A. *Ṭanhā*, or the unsatisfied desire for existence. The being having done that for which he must be rewarded or punished in future, and having *Ṭanhā*, will have a rebirth through the influence of Karma.

---

[1] The "soul" here criticised is the equivalent of the Greek *psyche*. The word "material" covers other states of matter than that of the physical body.

233. Q. *What is it that is born ?*

A. A new aggregation of *Skanḍhas*, or personality[1] caused by the last generative thought of the dying person.

---

[1]Upon reflection, I have substituted "personality" for "individuality" as written in the first edition. The successive appearance upon one or many earths, or "descents into generation", of the *tanhaically*-coherent parts (*Skhanḍhas*) of a certain being are a succession of personalities. In each birth the *personality* differs from that of the previous, or next succeeding birth. Karma the *deus ex machina*, masks (or shall we say reflects ?) itself, now in the personality of a sage, again as an artisan, and so on throughout the string of births. But though personalities ever shift, the one line of life along which they are strung like beads, runs unbroken, it is ever *that particular line*, never any other. It is therefore individual—an individual vital undulation—which is careering through the objective side of Nature, under the impulse of Karma and the creative direction of *Ṭanhā* and persists through many cyclic changes. Professor Rhys-Davids calls that which passes from personality to personality along the individual chain, "character" or "doing". Since "character" is not a mere metaphysical abstraction, but the sum of one's mental qualities and moral propensities, would it not help to dispel what Professor Rhys-Davids calls "the desperate expedient of a mystery " (*Buḍḍhism*, p. 101), if we regarded the life-undulation as individuality and each of its series of natal manifestations as a separate personality ? We *must* have two words to distinguish between the concepts, and find now so clear and expressive as the two I have chosen. The perfected individual, Buḍḍhistically speaking, is a Buḍḍha, I should say ; for a Buḍḍha is but the rare flower of humanity, without the least supernatural admixture. And, as countless generations—"four *asankheyyas* and a hundred thousand cycles" (Fausboll and Rhys-David's *Buḍḍhist Birth Stories*, No. 13)—are required to develop a man into a Buḍḍha, and *the iron will to become one runs throughout all the successive births*, what shall we call that which thus wills and perseveres ? *Character*, or individuality ? An individuality, but partly manifested in any one birth, built up of fragments from all the births.

The denial of "Soul" by Buḍḍha (see *Samyuṭṭa Nikāya*, the *Suṭṭa Piṭaka*) points to the prevalent delusive belief in an independent personality ; an entity, which after one birth would go to a

234. Q. *How many Skanḍhas are there* ?

A. Five .

235. Q. *Name the five Skanḍhas* ?

A. *Rūpa, Vedanā, Saññā, Samkhārā*, and *Vinnana.*

236. Q. *Briefly explain what they are* ?

A. *Rūpa*, material qualities ; *Vedanā*, sensation ; *Saññā*, abstract ideas ; *Samkhārā*, tendencies of mind ; *Viññāna*, mental powers, or consciousness. Of these we are formed ; by them we are conscious of existence ; and through them communicate with the world about us.

---

fixed place or state where, as a perfect entity, it could eternally enjoy or suffer. And what he shows is that the "I am I" consciousness, is as regards permanency, logically impossible, since its elementary constituents constantly change and the "I" of one birth differs from the "I" of every other births. But every thing that I have found in Buddhism accords with the theory of a gradual evolution of the perfected man—*viz.*, a Buddha—through numberless natal experiences. And in the consciousness of that individual man—*viz.*, a Buddha — through numberless natal experiences. And in the consciousness of that individual who, at the end of a given chain of births, attains Buḍḍhahood, or who succeeds in attaining the fourth stage of Dhyāna, or mystic self-development, in any of his births anterior to the final one, the scene of all these serial births are perceptible. In the *Jātakaṭṭhavaṅṅana*—so well translated by Professor Rhys-Davids—an expression continually recurs which, I think, rather supports such an idea *viz.* : "Then the Blessed One *made manifest an occurrence hidden by change of birth*", or "that which had been hidden by," etc. Early Buddhism then clearly held to a permanency of records in the Ākasha, and the potential capacity of man to read the same when he has evolved to the stage of true individual enlightenment. At death, and convulsions and trance, the *javana chitta* is transferred to the object last created by the desires. The will to live brings all thoughts into objectivity.

6–

237. Q. *To what cause must we attribute the differences in the combination of the five Skhandhas which make every individual differ from every other individual ?*

A. To the ripened Karma of the individual in his preceding births.

238. Q. *What is the force, or energy that is at work under the guidance of Karma, to produce the new being ?*

A. *Tanhā*—the will to *live* [1].

239. . *Upon what is the doctrine of rebirths founded ?*

A. Upon the perception that perfect justice, equilibrium and adjustment are inherent in the universal system of Nature. Buddhists do not believe that one life—even though it were extended to one hundred or five hundred years—is long enough for the reward or punishment of a man's deeds. The great circle of rebirths will be more or less quickly run through according to the preponderating purity or impurity of the several lives of the individual.

---

[1] The student may profitably consult Schopenhauei in this connection. Arthur Schopenhauer, a modern German philosopher of the most eminent ability, taught that "the Principle or Radical, of Nature, and of all her objects, the human body included is, intrinsically what we ourselves are the most conscious of in our own body, *viz.*, Will. Intellect is a secondary capacity of the primary will, a function of the brain in which this will reflects itself as Nature and object and body, as in a mirror......Intellect is secondary, but may lead, in saints, to a complete renunciation of will, as far as it urges "life" and is then extinguished in Nirvana (L. A. Sanders in *The Theosophist* for May 1882, p. 213).

240. Q. *Is this new aggregation of Skandhas—this new personality—the same being as that in the previous birth, Tanhā shoes has brought it into existence* ?

A. In one sense it is a new being ; in another it is not. In Pāli it is—"*nacha so nacha añño*," which means not the same nor yet another. During this life the *Skhandhas* are constantly changing ; and while the man A. B., of forty, is identical, as regards personality, with the youth A. B., of eighteen, yet, by the continual waste and reparation of his body, and change of mind and character, he is a different being. Nevertheless, the man in his old age justly reaps the reward of suffering consequent upon his thoughts and actions at every previous stage of his life. So the new being of a rebirth being the same individuality as before, but with a change, form, or new aggregation of *Skandhas*, justly reaps the consequences of his actions and thoughts in the previous existence.

241. Q. *But the aged man remembers the incidents of his youth, despite his being physically and mentally changed. Why, then, is not the recollection of past lives brought over by us from our last birth, into the present birth* ?

A. Because memory is included within the *Skandhas ;* and the *Skandhas* having changed with the new reincarnation, a new memory, the record of the particular existence, develops. Yet the record or re flection of all the past earth-lives must survive ; for when Prince Siḍḍhārtha became Buḍḍha, the full sequence of his previous births was seen by him. If their

[1] Physiologically speaking, man's body is completely changed every seven years.

several incidents had left no trace behind, this could not have been so, as there would have been nothing for him to see. And any one who attains to the fourth state of *Dhyāna* (psychical insight) can thus retrospectively trace the line of his lives.

242. Q. *What is the ultimate point towards which tend all these series of changes in form* ?

A. Nirvāṇa.

243. Q. *Does Buddhism teach that we should do good with the view of reaching Nirvana* ?

A. No ; that would be as absolute selfishness as though the reward hoped for had been money, a throne, or any other sensual enjoyment. Nirvāṇa cannot be so reached, and the unwise speculator is foredoomed to disappointment.

244. Q. *Please make it a little clearer* ?

A. Nirvāṇa is the synonym of unselfishnes, the entire surrender of selfhood to truth. The ignorant man aspires to nirvāṇic happiness without the least idea of its nature. Absence of selfishness is Nirvāṇa. Doing good with the view to getting results, or leading the holy life with the objects of gaining heavenly happiness, is not the Noble Life that the Buḍḍha enjoined. Without hope of reward the Noble life should be lived, and that is the highest life. The nirvāṇic state can be attained while one is living on this earth.

245. Q. *Name the ten great obstacles to advancement, called Sanyojanas, the Fetters* ?

A. Delusion of self (*Sakkāya-ditthi*) ; Doubt (*Vicikicchā*) ; Dependence on superstitious rites (*Silabbata-parāmāsa*) ; Sensuality, bodily passions (*Kāma* ;)

Hatred, ill-feeling (*Patigha*) ; Love of life on earth (*Rūparāga*) ; Desire for life in a heaven (*Arūparāga*) ; Pride (*Māna*) ; Self-righteousness (*Uḍḍhacca*) ; Ignorance (*Avijjā*).

246. Q. *To become an Arhaṭ, how many of these fetters must be broken ?*

A. All.

247. Q. *What are the five Niwāranas or Hindrances ?*

A. Greed, Malice, Sloth, Pride, and Doubt.

248. Q. *Why do we see this minute division of feelings, inpulses, workings of the mind, obstacles and aids to advancement so much used in the Buḍḍha's teachings ? It is very confusing to a beginner.*

A. It is to help us to obtain knowledge of ourselves, by training our minds to think out every subject in detail. By following out this system of self-examination, we come finally to acquire knowledge and see truth as it is. This is the course taken by every wise teacher to help his pupil's mind to develop.

249. Q. *How many of the Buḍḍha's disciples were specially renowned for their superior qualities ?*

A. There are eighty so distinguished. They are called the *Asīṭi Mahā Sāvakas.*

250. Q. *What did the Buḍḍha's wisdom embrace ?*

A. He knew the nature of the Knowable and the Unknowable, the Possible and the Impossible, the cause of Merit and Demerit ; he could read the thoughts of all beings ; he knew the laws of Nature, the illusions of the senses and the means to suppress desires ; he could distinguish the birth and rebirth of individuals, and other things.

251. Q. *What do we call the basic principle on which the whole of the Buḍḍha's teaching is constructed ?*

A. It is called *Paticca Samuppāḍā.*[1]

252. Q. *Is it easily grasped ?*

A. It is most difficult ; in fact, the full meaning and extent of it is beyond the capacity of such as are not perfectly developed.

253. Q. *What said the great commentator Buḍḍha Ghoṣha about it ?*

A. That even he was as helpless in this vast ocean of thought as one who is drifting on the ocean of waters.

254. Q. *Then why should the Buḍḍha say, in the Parinibbāna Suṭṭa, that he "has no such thing as the closed first of a teacher, who keeps something back" If his whole teaching was open to every one's comprehension why should so great and learned a man as Buḍḍha Ghoṣha declare it so hard to understand ?*

---

1 This fundamental or basic principle may be designated in Pāil *Niḍāna*—chain of causation or, literally, "Origination of dependence." Twelve *Niḍānas* are specified, *viz.*, : *Avijjā*—ignorance of the truth of natural religion ; *Samkhāra*—causal action, karma ; *Viññāna*—consciousness of personality, the "I am I" ; *Nāma rūpa*—name and form : *Salayatana*—six senses ; *Phassa*—contact ; *Vedanā*—feeling ; *Tanhā*—desire for enjoyment ; *Upāḍāna*—clinging ; *Bhava*—individualising existence ; *Jāti*—birth, caste ; *Jarā, marana, sokhaparideva, dukka, domanassa, upāyāsa*—decay, death, grief, lamentation, despair.

A. The Buḍḍha evidently meant that he taught everything freely ; but equally certain is it that the real basis of the Ḍharma can only be understood by him who has perfected his powers of comprehension. It is, therefore, incomprehensible to common, unenlightened persons.

255. Q. *How does the teaching of the Buḍḍha support this view ?*

A. The Buḍḍha looked into the heart of each person, and preached to suit the individual temperament and spiritual development of the hearer.

PART III

THE SANGHA

256. Q. *How do Buḍḍhist Bhikkhus differ from the priests of other religious ?*

A. In other religions the priests claim to be intercessors between men and God, to help to obtain pardon of sins ; the Buddhist Bhikkhus do not acknowledge or expect anything from a divine power.

257. Q. *But why then was it worth while to create this Order, or Brotherhood, or Society, apart from the whole body of the people, if they were not to do what other religious orders do ?*

A. The object in view was to cause the most virtuous, intelligent, unselfish and spiritually-minded persons to withdraw from the social surroundinge where their sensual and other selfish desires wers naturally strengthened, devote their lives to the acquisition of the highest wisdom, and fit themselves to teach and guide others out of the pleasant path leading towards misery, into the harder path that leads to true happiness and final liberation.

258. Q. *Besides the Eight, what two additional observances are obligatory upon the Bhikkhus ?*

A. I observe the precept to abstain from dancing, singing and unbecoming shows.

I observe the precept to abstain from receiving gold or silver.

The whole *Dasa*, or *Bhikkhu Sīla* or Ten Precepts, are binding on *all* Bhikkhus and *Samaneras*, or novices, but optional with lay devotees.

The *Atthanga Sīla* are for those who aspire to higher stages beyond the heavenly regions,[1] aspirants after Nirvāṇa.

259. Q. *Are there separate Rules and Precepts for the guidance and discipline of the Order ?*

A. Yes : there are 250, but all come under the following four heads :

Principal Disciplinary Rules (*Pāṭimokkha Samvara Sīla*).

Observances for the repression of the senses (*Inḍriya Samvara Sīla*).

Regulations for justly procuring and using food, diet, robes, etc., (*Paccaya Sannissiṭa Sīla*).

Directions for leading an unblemished life (*Ajivapari Suḍḍha Sīla*).

260. Q. *Enumerate some crimes and offences that Bhikkhus are particularly prohibited from committing ?*

A. Real Bhikkhus abstain from :

Destroying the life of beings ;

Stealing ;

False exhibition of "occult" powers to deceive anybody ;

Sexual intercourse ;

Falsehood ;

---

[1] The Upāsaka and Upāsika observes these on the Buḍḍhist *Uposatha* (Sabbath) days (in Skr. *Upavasa*). They are the 8th, 14th and 15th days of each half lunar month.

The use of intoxicating liquors, and eating at unseasonable times ;

Dancing, singing, and unbecoming shows ;
Using garlands, scents, perfumes, etc. ;

Using high and broad beds, couches or seats ; receiving presents of gold, silver, raw grain and meat, women, and maidens, slaves, cattle, elephants, etc. ;

Defaming ;
Using harsh and reproachful language ;
Idle talk ;
Reading and hearing fabulous stories and tales ;
Carrying messages to and from laymen ;
Buying and selling ;
Cheating, bribing, deception, and fraud ;
Imprisoning, plundering, and threatening others ;

The practice of certain specified magical arts and sciences, such as fortune-telling, astrological predictions, palmistry, and other sciences, that go under the name of magic. Any of these would retard the progress of one who aimed at the attainment of Nirvāṇa.

261. *Q. What are the duties of Bhikkus to the laity?*

A. Generally, to set them an example of the highest morality ; to teach and instruct them ; to preach and expound the Law ; to recite the *Paritta* (comforting texts) to the sick, and publicly in times of public calamity, when requested to do so ; and unceasingly to exhort the people to virtuous actions. They should dissuade them from vice ; be compassionate and tender-hearted, and seek to promote the welfare of all beings.

262. Q. *What are the rules for admission into the Order?*

A. The candidate is not often taken before his tenth year ; he must have the consent of his parents ; be free from leprosy, boils, consumption and fits ; be a free man ; have no debts ; and must not be a criminal or deformed or in the royal service.

263. Q. *As a novice what is he called ?*

A. *Samanera*, a pupil.[1]

264. Q. *At what age can a Samanera be ordained as Sramana—monk ?*

A. Not before his twentieth year.

265. Q. *When ready for ordination what happens ?*

A. At a meeting of Bhikkhus he is presented by a Bhikkhu as his proposer, who reports that he is qualified, and the candidate says : "I ask the Saṅgha, Reverend Sirs, for the *Upasampaḍa* (ordination) ceremony, etc."

His introducer then recommends that he be admitted. He is then accepted.

266. Q. *What then ?*

A. He puts on the robes and repeats the Three Refuges (*Tisarana*) and Ten Precepts (*Ḍasa Sila*).

267. Q. *What are the two essentials to be observed ?*

A. Poverty and Chastity. A Bhikkhu before ordination must possess eight things, *viz.*, his robes, a

---

1 The relationship his to Guru, or teacher, is almost like that of godson to godfather among Christians, only more real, for the teacher becomes father, mother, family and all to him.

girdle for his loins, a begging-bowl, water-strainer, razor, needle, fan, sandals. Within limitations strictly specified in the *Vināya*, he may hold certain other properties.

268. Q. *What about the public confession of faults* ?

A. Once every fortnight, a *Paṭimokka* (Disburdenment) ceremony is performed, when every Bhikkhu confesses to the assembly such faults as he has committed and takes such penances as may be prescribed.

269. Q. *What daily routine must he follow* ?

A. He rises before daylight, washes, sweeps the vihāra, sweeps around the Bo-tree that grows near every vihāra, brings the drinking-water for the day and filters it ; retires for meditation, offers flowers before the dāgoba, or relic-mound, or before the Bo-tree ; then takes his begging-bowl and goes from house to house collecting food—which he must not ask for, but receive in his bowl as given voluntarily by the householders. He returns, bathes his feet and eats, after which he resumes meditation.

270. Q. *Must we believe that there is no merit in the offering of flowers (mala pūjā) as an act of worship* ?

A. That act itself is without merit as a mere formality ; but if one offers a flower as the sweetest, purest expression of heartfelt reverence for a holy being then, indeed, is the offering an act of ennobling worship.

271. Q. *What next does the Bhikkhu do* ?

A. He pursues his studies. At sunset he again sweeps the sacred places, lights a lamp, listens to the instructions of his superior, and confesses to him any fault he may have committed.

272. Q. *Upon what are his four earnest meditations (Sati-pātthāna) made* ?

A. 1. On the body, *Kayānapassana.*

2. On the feeling, *Vedanānupassānā.*

3. On the mind, *Chittānupassānā.*

4. On the doctrine, *Ḍhammanupassānā*

273. Q. *What is the aim of the four Great Efforts (Sammappaḍhānā)* ?

A. To suppress one's animal desires and grow in goodness.

272. Q. *For the perception by the Bhikkhu of the highest truth, is reason said to be the best, or intuition* ?

A. Intuition—a mental state in which any desired truth is inst antaneously grasped.

275. Q. *And when can that development be reached* ?

A. When one, by the practice of *Jñāna,* comes to its fouth stage of unfolding.

275. Q. *Are we to believe that in the final stage of Jñāna, and in the condition called Samāḍhi, the mind is a blank and thought is arrested* ?

A. Quite the contrary. It is then that one's consciousness is most intensely active, and one's power. to gain knowledge correspondingly vast.

277. Q. *Try to give me a simile* ?

A. In the ordinary waking state one's view of knowledge is as limited as the sight of a man who walks on a road between high hills ; in the higher consciousness of *Jñāna* and *Samāḍhi* it is like the sight of the eagle poised in the upper sky and overlooking a whole country.

278. Q. *What do our books say about the Buḍḍha's use of this faculty ?*

A. They tell us that it was his custom, every morning, to glance over the world and, by his divine (clairvoyant)sight, see where there were persons ready to rteceive the truth.He would then contrive, if possible, that it should reach them. When persons visited him he would look into their minds, read their secret motives, and then preach to them according to their needs.

PART IV

THE RISE AND SPREAD OF BUDDHISM

279. Q. *As regards the number of its followers, how does Buḍḍhism at this date compare with the other chief religions ?*

A. The followers of the Buḍḍha Dharma outnumber those of every other religion.

280. Q. *What is the estimated number ?*

A. About five hundred millions (5,000 lakhs or 500 crores) : this is five-thirteenths, or not quite half, of the estimated population of the globe.

281. Q. *Have many great battles been fought and many countries conquered ; has much human blood been split to spread the Buḍḍha Ḍharma ?*

A. History does not record one of those cruelties and crimes as having been committeed to propagate our religion. Sɔ far as we know, it has not caused the spilling of a drop of blood. (See foot-note *ante*—Professor Kolb's testimony.)

282. Q. *What, them, is the secret of its wonderful spread ?*

A. It can be nothing else than its intrinsic excellence : its self-evident basis of truth, its sublime moral teaching, and its suffidiency for all human needs.

283. Q. *How has it been propagated ?*

A. The Buḍḍha, during the forty-five years of his life as a Teacher, travelled widely in India and preach the Dharma. He sent his wisest and best disciples to do the same throughout India.

284. Q. *When did He send for his pioneer missionaries ?*

A. On the full-moon day of the month *Wap* (October).

285. Q. *What did he tell them ?*

A. He called them together and said : "Go forth, Bhikkhus, go and preach the law to the world. Work for the good of others as well as for your own .... Bear ye the glad tidings to every man. Let no two of you take the same way."

286. Q. *How long before the Christian era did this happen ?*

A. About six centuries.

287. Q. *What help did Kings give ?*

A. Besides the lower classes, great Kings, Rājās and Mahārājās were converted and gave their influence to spread the religion.

288. Q. *What about pilgrims ?*

A. Learned pilgrims came in different centuries to India and carried back with them books and teachings to their native lands. So, gradually, whole nations forsook their own faiths and became Buḍḍhists.

289. Q. *To whom, more than to any other person, is the world indebted for the permanent establishment of Buḍḍha's religion ?*

A. To the Emperor Ashoka, surnamed the Great, sometimes Piyaḍāsi, sometimes Ḍharmāshoka. He was the son of Binḍusāra, King of Magaḍha, and grandson of Chanḍragupṭa, who drove the Greeks out of India.

290. Q. *When did he reign ?*

A. In the third century B.C., about two centuries after the Buḍḍha's time. Historians disagree as to his exact date, but not very greatly.

291. Q. *What made him great ?*

A. He was the most powerful monarch in Indian history, as warrior and as statesman ; but his noblest characteristics were his love of truth and justice, tolerance of religious differences, equity of government, kindness to the sick, to the poor, and to animals. His name is revered from Siberia to Ceylon.

292. Q. *Was he born a Buḍḍhist ?*

A. No, he was converted in the tenth year after his anointment as King, by Nigroḍha Samanera, an Arhaṭ.

293. Q. *What did he do for Buḍḍhism ?*

A. He drove out bad Bhikkus, encouraged good ones, built monasteries and dàgobas everywhere, established gardens, opened hospitals for men and animals, convened a council at Patna to revise and re-establish the Ḍharma, promoted female religious education, and sent embassies to five Greek kings, his allies, and to all the sovereigns of India, to preach the doctrines of the Buḍḍha. It was he who built the monuments at Kapilàvasṭu, Buḍḍha Gàya, Isipatana and Kusinàrà, our four chief places of pilgrimage, besides thousands more.

294. Q. *What absolute proofs exist as to his noble character ?*

A. Within recent years there have been discovered, in all parts of India, fourteen Edicts of his, inscribed on living rocks, and eight on pillars erected by his orders. They fully prove him to have been one of the wisest and most high-minded sovereigns who ever lived.

295. Q. *What character do these inscriptions give to Buḍḍhism ?*

A. They show it to be a religion of noble tolerence, of universal brotherhood, of righteousness and justice. It has no taint of selfishness, sectarianism or intolerence. They have done more than anything else to win for it the respect in which it is now held by the great pandiṭs of western countries.

296. Q. *What most precious gift did Ḍharmàshoka make to Buḍḍhism ?*

A. He gave his beloved son, Mahinda, and daughter, Saṅghamiṭṭa, to the Order, and sent them to Ceylon to introduce the religion.

297. Q. *Is this fact recorded in the history of Ceylon?*

A. Yes, it is all recorded in the *Mahàvansa*, by the keepers of the royal records, who were then living and saw the missionaries.

298. Q. *Is there some proof of Saṅghamiṭṭa's mission still visible ?*

A. Yes ; she brought with her to Ceylon a branch of the very Boḍhi under which the Buḍḍha. sat when he became Enlightened, and it is still growing.

299. Q. *Where ?*

A. At Anuràḍhapura. The history of it has been officially preserved to the present time. Planted in 306 B.C., it is the oldest historical tree in the world

300. Q. *Who was the reigning sovereign at that time ?*

A. Ḍēvanampiyaṭissa. His consort, Queen Anula, had invited Saṅghamiṭṭa to come and establish the Bhikkhuni branch of the Order.

301. Q. *Who came with Saṅghamiṭṭa ?*

A. Many other Bhikkunis. She, in due time, admitted the Queen and many of her ladies, together with five hundred virgins, into the Order.

302. Q. *Can we trace the effects of the foreign work of the Emperor Ashoka's missionaries ?*

A. His son and daughter introduced Buḍḍhism into Ceylon : his monks gave it to the whole of Northern India, to fourteen Indian nations outside its boundaries, and to five Greek kings, his allies, with whom he made treaties to admit his religious preachers

303. Q. *Can you name them ?*

A. ANTIOCHUS of Syria, PTOLEMY of Egypt, ANTIGONUS OF Macedon, MERGAS of Cyrene, and ALEXANDER of Epidos.

304. Q. *Where do we learn this ?*

A. From the Edicts themselves of Ashoka the Great, inscribed by him on rocks and stone pillars, which are still standing and can be seen by everybody who chooses to visit the places.

305. Q. *Through what western religious brother hoods did the Buḍḍha Ḍharma mingle itself with western thought ?*

A. Through the sects of the Therapeuts of Egypt and the Essenes of Palestine.

306. Q. *When were Buḍḍhist books first introduced into China ?*

A. As early as the second or third century B.C. Five of Ḍharmāshoka's monks are said—in the *Samanta Pasāḍika* and the *Sārattha Ḍīpanī*—Two Pālī books—to have been sent to the five divisions of China.

307. Q. *Whence and when did it reach Korea ?*

A. From China, in the year A.D. 372.

308. Q. *Whence and when did it reach Japan ?*

A. From Korea, in A.D. 552.

309. Q. *Whence and when did it reach Cochin, China Formosa, Java, Mongolia, Yorkand, Balk, Bokhara, Afghanistan and other Central Asian countries ?*

A. Apparently in the fourth and fifth centuries A.D.

310. Q. *From Ceylon, whither and when did it spread ?*

A. To Burma, in A.D. 450, and thence gradually into Arakan, Kamboja and Pegu. In the seventh century (A.D. 638) it spread to Siam, where it is now, as it has been always since then, the State religion.

311. Q. *From Kashmir, where else did it spread besides to China ?*

A. To Nepāl and Tibet.

312. Q. *Why is it that Buḍḍhism, which was once the prevailing religion throughout India, now almost extinct there ?*

A. Buddhism was at first pure and noble, the very teaching of the Ṭatḥagaṭa ; its Sangha were virtuous and observed the Precepts ; it won all hearts and spread joy through many nations, as the morning light sends life through the flowers. But after some centuries, bad Bhikkhus got ordination (*Upasampada*) the Sangha became rich, lazy, and sensual the, Dharma was corrupted, and the Indian nation abandoned it.

313. Q. *Did anything happen about the ninth or tenth century A.D. to hasten its downfall ?*

A. Yes.

314. Q. *Anything besides the decay of spirituality the corruption of the Saṅgha, and the reaction of the populace from a higher ideal of man to unintelligent idolatry ?*

A. Yes. It is said that the Mussalmāns invaded, overran and conquered large areas of India ; everywhere doing their utmost to stamp out our religion.

315. Q. *What cruel acts are they charged with doing ?*

A. They burnt, pulled down or otherwise destroyed our vihāras, slaughtered our Bhikkhus, and consumed with fire our religious books.

316. Q. *Was our literature completely destroyed in India ?*

A. No. Many Bhikkhus fled across the borders into Tibet and other safe places of refuge, carrying their books with them.

317. Q. *Have any traces of these books been recently discovered ?*

A. Yes. Rai Bhānur Saraṭ Chandra Dās, C.I.E., a noted Bengali paṇdit, saw hundreds of them in the vihāra libraries of Tibet, brought copies of some of the most important back with him, and is now employed by the Government of India in editing and publishing them.

318. Q. *In which country have we reason to believe the sacred books of primitive Buḍḍhism have been best preserved and least corrupted ?*

A. Ceylon. The *Encyclopaedia Britannaica* says that in this island Buḍḍhism has, for specified reasons, " retained almost its pristine purity to modern times."

319. Q. *Has any revision of the text of the Pitakas been made in modern times ?*

A. Yes. A careful revision of the Vinaya Pitaka was made in Ceylon in the year A.D. 1875, by a convention of the most learned Bhikkhus, under the presidency of H. Sumaṅgala, Praḍhāna Sṭhavira.

320. Q. *Has there been any friendly intercourse in the interest of Buḍḍhism between the peoples of the Southern and those of the Northern Buḍḍhist countries ?*

A. In the year A.D. 1891, a successful attempt was made to get the Praḍhāna Nayakas of the two great divisions to agree to accept fourteen propositions as embodying fundamental Buddhistic beliefs recognised and taught by both divisions. These propositions, drafted by Colonel Olcott, were carefully translated into Burmese, Sinhalese and Japanese, discussed one by one, unanimously adopted and signed by the chief monks, and published in January 1892.

321. Q. *With what good result* ?

A. As the result of the good understanding now existing, a number of Japanese bhikkhus and sạmaneras have been sent to Ceylon and India to study Pāli and Samskṛṭ.

322. Q. *Are there signs that the Buḍḍha Dharma is growing in favour in non-Buḍḍhistic countries* ?[1]

A. There are. Translations of our more valuable books are appearing, many articles in reviews, magazines and newspapers are being published, and excellent original treatises by distinguished writers are coming from the press. Moreover, Buddhist and non-Buddhist lecturers are publicly discoursing on Buddhism to large audiences in western countries. The Shin Shu sect of Japanese Buḍḍhist have actually opened missions at Honolulu, San Francisco, Sacramento and other American places.

323. Q. *What two leading ideas of ours are chiefly taking hold upon the western mind* ?

A. Those of Karma and Reincarnation. The rapiḍity of their acceptance is very surprising.

324. Q. *What is believed to be the explanation of this* ?

A. Their appeals to the natural instinct of justice, and their evident reasonableness.

1/ See Appendix.

PART V

BUDDHISM AND SCIENCE

325. Q. *Has Buḍḍhism any right to be considered a scientific religion, or may it be classified its a " revealed " one ?*

A. Most emphatically it is not a revealed religion. The Buḍḍha did not so preach, nor is to be so understood. On the contrary, he gave it out as the statement of eternal truths, which his predecessors had taught like himself.

326. Q. *Repeat again the name of thẽ suṭṭa, in which the Buḍḍha tells us not to believe in an alleged revelation without testing it by one's reason and experience ?*

A. The *Kālāma Suṭṭa,* of the *Angutthara Nikaya.*

327. Q. *Do Buḍḍhists accept the theory that everything has been formed out of nothing by a Creator ?*

A. The Buḍḍha taught that two things are causeless; *viz.,* Ākāsha, and Nirvāṇa. Everything has come out of Ākāsha, in obedience to a law of motion inherent in it, and, after a certain existence, passes away. Nothing ever came out of nothing. We do not believe in miracles ; hence we deny creation, and cannot conceive of a creation of something out of nothing. Nothing organic is eternal. Everything is in a state of constant flux, and undergoing change and reformation, keeping up the continuity according to the law of evolution.

328. Q. *Is Buḍḍhism opposed to education, and to the study of science ?*

A. Quite the contrary : in the *Sigālowāda Suṭṭa* in a discourse preached by the Buḍḍha, He specified as one of the duties of a teacher that he should give his pupils " instruction in science and lore ". The Buḍḍha's higher teachings are for the enlightened, the wise, and the thoughtful.

329. Q. *Can you show any further endorsement of Buḍḍhism by science ?*

A. The Buḍḍha's doctrine teaches that there were many progenitors of the human race ; also there there is a principle of differentiation among men ; certain individuals have a greater capacity for the rapid attainment of Wisdom and arrival at Nirvāṇā than others.

330. Q. *Any other ?*

A. Buḍḍhism supports the teaching of the indestructibility of force.

331. Q. *Should Buḍḍhism be called a chart of science or a code of morals ?*

A. Properly speaking, a pure moral philosophy, a system of ethics and transcendental metaphysics. It is so eminently practical that the Buddha kept silent when Malunkya asked about the origin of thing .

332. Q. *Why did he do that ?*

A. Because he thought that our chief aim should be to see things as they exist around us and try to make them better, not to waste time in intellectual speculations.

333. Q. *What do Buḍḍhists say is the reason for the occasional birth of very good and wise children of bad parents, and that of very bad ones of good parents ?*

A. It is beeause of the respective Karmas of children and parents ; each may have deserved that such unusual relationships should be formed in the present birth.

334. Q. *Is anything said about the body of the Buddha giving out a bright light ?*

A. Yes, there was a divine radiance sent forth from within by the power of his holiness.

335. Q. *What is it called in Pālī ?*

A. *Buddharansi*, the Buddha rays.

336. Q. *How many colours could be seen in it ?*

A. Six, linked in pairs.

337. Q. *Their names ?*

A. *Nīla, Piṭa, Lohiṭa, Avadaṭa, Mangesṭḍ, Prabhasvra.*

338. Q. *Did other persons emit such shining light ?*

A. Yes, all Arhats did and, in fact, the light shines stronger and brighter in proportion to the spiritual development of the person.

339. Q. *Where do we see these colours represented ?*

A. In all vihāras where there are painted images of the Buḍḍha. They are also seen in the stripes of the Buḍḍhist Flag, first made in Ceylon but now widely adopted throughout Buddhist countries.

340. Q. *In which discourse does the Buḍḍha himself speak of this shining about him ?*

A. In the *Mahā-Prainibbana Suṭṭō*, Ānanḍa his favourite disciple, noticing the great splendour which came from his Master's body, the Buḍḍha said that on two occasions this extraordinary shining occurs, (*a*) just after a Ṭaṭhāgaṭa gains the supreme insight, and (*b*) on the night when he passes finally away.

341. Q. *Where do we read of this great brightness being emitted from the body of another Buḍḍha ?*

A. In the story of Sumeḍha and Dipānkāra Buḍḍha, found in the *Niḍanakathā* of the *Jāṭaka* book, or story of the reincarnations of the Bodhisaṭṭva Sidḍhārṭha Gauṭama.

342. Q. *How is it described ?*

A. As a halo of a fathom's depth.

343. *What do the Hinḍus call it ?*

A. Ṭ*ejas,* its extended radiance they call *Prākāsha.*

344. Q. *What do Europeans call it now ?*

A. The human aura.

345. Q. *What great scientist has proved the existence of this aura by carefully conducted experiments ?*

A. The Baron Von Reichenbach. His experiments are fully described in his *Researches,* published in 1844-5. Dr. Baraduc, of Paris, has, quite recently, photographed this light.

346. Q. *Is this bright aura a miracle or a natural phenomenon ?*

A. Natural. It has been proved that not only all human beings but animals, trees, plants and even stones have it.

347. Q. *What peculiarity has it in the case of a Buḍḍha or an Arahaṭ ?*

A. It is immensely brighter and more extended than in cases of other beings and objects. It is the evidence of their superior developments in the power of *Iḍḍhi*. The light has been seen coming from dāgabos in Ceylon where relics of the Buḍḍha are said to be enshrined.

348. Q. *Do people of other religions besides Buḍḍhism and Hinḍūism also believe in this light ?*

A. Yes, in all pictures of Christian artists this light is represented as shining about the bodies of their holy personages. The same belief is found to have existed in other religions.

349. Q. *What historical incident supports the modern theory of hypnotic suggestion ?*

A. That of Chullapanthaka, as told in the Pāli Commentary on the *Dhammapaḍa*, etc.

350. Q. *Give me the facts.*

A. He was a bhikkhu who became an Arhaṭ. On that very day the Buḍḍha sent a messenger to call him. When the man reach the Vihāra, he saw three hundred bhikkhus in one group, each exactly like the others in every respect. On his asking which was Chullapanthaka, every one of the three hundred figures replied : "I am Chullapanthaka."

351. Q. *What did the messenger do?*

A. In his confusion he returned and reported to the Buḍḍha.

352. Q. *What did the Buḍḍha then tell him ?*

A. To return to the vihāra and, if the same thing happened, to catch by the arm the *first* figure who said he was Chullapanthaka and lead him to him. The Buḍḍha knew that the new Arhaṭ would make this display of his acquired power to impress illusionary pictures of himself upon the messenger.

353. Q. *What is this power of illusion called in Pālī ?*

A. *Manomaya Iḍḍhī.*

354. Q. *Were the illusionary copies of the Arahaṭ's person material ? Were they composed of substance and could they have been full and handled by the messenger ?*

A. No ; they were pictures impressed by his thought and trained will-power upon the messenger's mind.

355. Q. *To what would you compare them ?*

A. To a man's reflection in a mirror being exactly like him yet without solidity.

356. Q. *To make such an illusion on the messenger's mind, what was necessary ?*

A. That Chullapanthaka should clearly conceive in his own mind his exact appearance, and then impress that, with as many duplicates or repetitions as he chose, upon the sensitive brain of the messenger.

357. Q. *What is this process now called ?*

A. Hypnotic Suggestion.

358. Q. *Could any third party have also seen these illusionary figures ?*

A. That would depend on the will of the Arhaṭ or hypnotiser.

359. Q. *What do you mean ?*

A. Supposing that fifty or five hundred persons were there, instead of one, the Arhaṭ could will that the illusion should be seen by all alike ; or, if he chose, he could will that the mesenger should be the-only one to see them.

360. Q. *Is this branch of science well known in our day ?*

A. Very well known ; it is familiar to all students of mesmerism and hypnotism.

361. Q. *In what does our modern scientific belief support the theory of Karma, as taught in Buddhism ?*

A. Modern scientists teach that every generation of men is heir to the cosequences of the virtues and the vices of the preceding generation, not in the mass, as such, but in every individual case. Every one of us, according to Buddhism, gets a birth which represents the causes generated by him in an antecedent birth. This is the idea of Karma.

362. Q. *What says the Vāsettha Suṭṭa about the causation in Nature ?*

A. It says : "The world exists by cause ; all things exist by cause ; all beings are bound by cause.'

363. Q. *Does Buḍḍhism teach the unchangeableness of the visible universe ; our earth, the sun, the moon, the stars, the mineral, vegetable, animal and human kingdoms ?*

A. No. It teaches that all are constantly changing, and all must disappear in course of time.

364. Q. *Never to reappear ?*

A. Not so : the principle of evolution, guided by Karma, individual and collective, will evolve another universe with its contents, as our universe was evolved out of the Ākāsha.

365. Q. *Does Buddhism admit that man has in his nature any latent powers for the production of phenomena commonly called "miracles"?*

A. Yes; but they are natural, not supernatural. They may be developed by a certain system which laid down in our sacred books, *Visuḍḍhi Mārga* for instant.

366. Q. *What is this branch of sicence called?*

A. The Pali name is *Iḍḍhi-vidhanānā.*

367. Q. *How many kinds are there?*

A. Two: *Bāhira, i.e.*, one in which the phenomena-working power may be temporarily obtained by ascetic practices and also by resort to drugs, the recitation of *manṭras* (charms), or other extraneous aids; and *Sasaniks*, that in which the power in question is acquired by interior self-development, and covers all and more than the phenomena o. *Laukika Iḍḍhi.*

368. Q. *What class of men enjoy these powers?*

A. They gradually develop in one which pursues a certain course of ascetic practice called *Ḍhyāna.*

369. Q. *Can this Iḍḍhi power be lost?*[1]

A. The *Bāhira* can be lost, but the *Sasanika* never, when once acquired. *Lokoṭṭara* knowledge once

---

[1] Sumangala Sṭhavira explains to me that those transcendent powers are permanently possessed only by one who has subdued all the passions (*Klesa*), in other words, an Arhaṭ. The powers may be developed by a bad man and used for doing evil things, but their activity is but brief, the revellious passions again dcminat the sorcerer, and he becomes at last their victim.

obtained is never lost, and it is by this knowledge *only* that the absolute condition of Nirvāṇa is known by the Arhaṭ. And this knowledge can be got by following the noble life of the Eightfold Path.

370. Q. *Had Buḍḍha the Lokoṭṭara Iḍḍhī* ?

A. Yes, in perfection.

371. Q. *And his disciples also had it* ?

A. Yes, some but not all equally ; the capacity for acquiring these occult powers varies with the individual.

372. Q. *Give examples* ?

A. Of all the disciples of the Buḍḍha, Mogallāna was possessed of the most extraordinary powers for making phenomena, while Ānanḍa could develop none during the twenty-five years in which he was the personal and intimate disciple of the Buddha himself. Later he did, as the Buḍḍha had foretold he would.

373. Q. *Does a man acquire these powers suddenly or gradually* ?

A. Normally, they gradually develop themselves as the disciple progressively gains control over his lower nature in a series of births.[1]

374. Q. *Does Buḍḍhism pretend that the miracle of rasing those who are dead is possible* ?

A. No. The Buḍḍha teaches the contrary, in that beautiful story of Kisā Goṭamī and the mustard-

[1] When the powers suddenly show themselves, the inference is that the individual had developed himself in the next anterior birth. We do not believe in eccentric breaks in natural law.

seed. But when a person only seems to be dead but is not actually so, resuscitation is possible.

375. Q. *Give me an idea of these successive stages of the Lokoṭṭara development in Iḍḍhi ?*

A. There are six degrees attainable by Arhaṭs ; what is higher than them is to be reached only by a Buḍḍha.

376. Q. *Describe the six stages or degreses ?*

A. We may divide them into two groups of, three each. The first to include (1) Progressive retrospection, *viz.*, a gradually acquired power to look backward in time towards the origin of things ; (2) Progressive foresight, or power of prophecy ; (3) Gradual extinction of desires and attachments to material things.

377. Q. *What would the second group include ?*

A. The same faculties, but illimitably developed. Thus, the full Arhaṭ possesses perfect retrospection, perfect foresight, and has absolutely extinguished the last trace of desireand selfish attractions.

378. Q. *What the four means for obtaining Iḍḍhi ?*

A. The will its exertion, mental development, and discrimination between right and wrong.

379. Q. *Our Scriptures relate hundreds of instances of phenomena produced by Arhaṭs : what did you say was the name of this faculty or power ?*

A. *Iḍḍhi viḍha.* One possessing this can, by manipulating the forces of Nature, produce any wonderful phenomenon, *i. e.*, make any scientific experiment he chooses.

380. Q. *Did the Buḍḍha encourage displays of phenomena ?*

A. No ; he expressly discouraged them as tending to create confusion in the minds of those who were not acquainted with the principles involved. They also tempt their possessors to show them merely to gratify idle curiosity and their own vanity. Moreover, similar phenomena can be shown by magicians and sorcerers learned in the *Laukika,* or the baser form o *Iḍḍhī* science. All false pretensions to supernatural attainment by monks are among the unpardonable sins (*Tevijja Suṭṭa*).

381. Q. *You spoke of a " ḍeva " having appeared to the Prince Siḍḍhartha under a variety of forms ; what do Buddhists believe respecting races of elemental invisible beings having relations with mankind ?*

A. They believe that there are such beings who inhabit worlds or spheres of their own. The Buḍḍhist doctrine is that, by interior self-development and conquest over his baser nature, the Arhaṭ becomes superior to even the most formidable of the ḍevas, and may subject and control the lower orders.

382. Q. *How many kinds of ḍevas are there ?*

A. Three : *Kāmāvāchārā* (those who are still under the domination of the passions) ; *Rūpāvāchārā* (a higher class, which still retain an individual form) : *Arūpāvāchārā* (the highest in degree of purification, who are devoid of material forms).

383. Q. *Should we fear any of them* ?

A. He who is pure and compassionate in heart and of a courageous mind need fear nothing: no man, god, *brahmarakkhas,* demon or ḍeva, can injure him, but some have power to torment the impure, as well as those who invite their approach.

APPENDIX

THE following text of the fourteen items of belief which have been accepted as fundamental principles in both the Southern and Northern sections of Buḍḍhism, by authoritative committees to whom they were submitted by me personally, have so much historical importance that they are added to the present edition of THE BUḌḌHIST CATECHISM as an Appendix. It has very recently been reported to me by H. E. Prince Ouchtomsky, the learned Russian Orientalist, that having had the document translated to them, the Chief Lamas of the great Mongolian Buḍḍhist monasteries declared to him that they accept every one of the propositions as drafted, with the one exception that the date of the Buḍḍha is by them believed to have been some thousands of years earlier than the one given by me. This surprising fact had not hitherto come to my knowledge. Can it be that the Mongolian Saṅgha confuse the real epoch of Sākya Muni with that of his alleged next predecessor ? Be this as it may, it is a most encouraging fact that the whole Buḍḍhistic world may now be said to have united to the extent at least of these Fourteen Propositions.

H. S. O.

FUNDAMENTAL BUḌḌHISTIC BELIEFS

I Buḍḍhists are taught to show the same tolerance, forbearance, and brotherly love to all men, without distinction ; and an unswerving kindness towards the members of the animal kingdom.

II The universe was evolved, not created ; and its functions according to law, not according to the caprice of any God.

III The truths upon which Buḍḍhism is founded are natural. They have, we believe, been taught in successive kalpas, or world-periods, by certain illuminated beings called BUḌḌHAS, the name BUḌḌHA meaning "Enlightened".

IV The fourth Teacher in the present kalpa was Sākya Muni, or Gauṭama Buḍḍha, who was born in a Royal family in India about 2,500 years ago. He is an historical personage and his name was Siḍḍhārṭhā Gauṭama.

V Sākya Muni taught that ignorance produces desire, unsatisfied desire is the cause of rebirth, and rebirth, the cause of sorrow. To get rid of sorrow therefore, it is necessary to escape rebirth ; to escape rebirth, it necessary to extinguish desire ; and to extinguish desire, it is necessary to destroy ignorance.

VI Ignorance fosters the belief that rebirth is a necessary thing. When ignorance is destroyed the worthlessness of every such rebirth, considered as an end in itself, is perceived, as well as the paramount need of adopting a course of life by which the necessity for such repeated rebirths can be abolished. Ignorance also begets the illusive and illogical idea that there is only one existence for man, and the other illusion that this one life is followed by states of unchangeable pleasure or torment.

VII The dispersion of all this ignorance can be attained by the perservering preactice of an all embracing altruism in conduct, development of intelligence, wisdom in thought, and destruction of desire for the lower personal pleasures.

VIII The desire to live being the cause of rebirth, when that is extinguished rebirths cease and the perfected individual attains by meditation that highest state of peace called *Nirvāṇa.*

IX Sākya Muni taught that ignorance can be dispelled and sorrow removed by the knowledge of the four Noble Truths, *viz.* :

1. The miseries of existence ;
2. The cause productive of misery, which is the desire ever renewed of satisfying oneself without being able ever to secure that end ;
3. The destruction of that desire, or the estranging of oneself from it ;
4. The means of obtaining this destruction of desire. The means which he pointed out is called the Noble Eightfold Path, *viz.* : Right Belief ; Right Thought ; Right Speech ; Right Action ; Right Means of Livelihood ; Right Exertion ; Right Remembrance ; Right Meditation.

X Right Meditation leads to spiritual enlightenment, or the development of that Buḍḍha-like faculty which is latent in every man.

XI The essence of Buḍḍhism, as summed up by the Taṭhāgaṭhā (Buḍḍha) himself, as :—

To cease from all sin,

To get virtue,

To purifiy the heart.

XII The universe is subject to a natural causation known as "Karma". The merits and demerits of a being in past existences determine his condition in the present one. Each man, therefore, has prepared the causes of the effects which he now experiences.

XIII The obstacles to the attainment of good karma may be removed by the observance of the following precepts, which are embraced in the moral code of Buḍḍhism, *viz* : (1) Kill not ; (2) Steal not ; (3) Indulge in no forbidden sexual pleasure ; (4) Lie not ; (5) Take no intoxication or stupefying drug or liquor. Five other precepts which need not be here enumerated should be observed by those who would attain, more quickly than the average layman, the release from misery and rebirth.

XIV Buḍḍhism discourages superstitious credulity. Gauṭama Buḍḍha taught it to be the duty of a parent to have his child educated in science and literature. He also taught that no one should believe what is spoken by any sage, written in any book, or affirmed by tradition, unless it accord with reason.

Drafted as a common platform upon which all Buḍḍhists can agree.

H. S. OLCOTT, P.T.S.

Respectfully submitted for the approval of the High Priests of the nations which we severally represent, in the Buḍḍhist Conference held at Adyar, Madras, on the 8th, 9th, 10th, 11th, and 12th of January, 1891 (A.B. 2434).

Japan	..	Kozen Gunaratana Chiezo Tokuzawa
Burmah	..	U. Hmoay Tha Aung
Ceylon	..	Ḍhammapala Hevaviṭarana
The Maghs of Chittagong	..	Kṛshṇa Chanḍra Chowdry, by his appointed Proxy, Maung The Dwe.

BURMAH

Approved on behalf of the Buḍḍhists of Burmah, this 3rd day of February, 1891 (A.B. 2434) :

Tha-tha-na-baing Saydawgyi ; Aung Myi Shwebōn Sayadaw ; Me-ga-waddy Sayadaw ; Hmat-Khaya Sayadaw ; Hti-līn Sayadaw ; Myadaung Sayadaw ; Hla-Hvwe Sayadaw ; and sixteen others.

CEYLON

Approved on behalf of the Buḍḍhists of Ceylon this 25th day of February, 1891 (A. B. 2434 ; Mahanuwara upawasatha Puspārāma vihārāḍhipāṭi Hippola Ḍhamma Rakkhiṭa Sɔbhiṭabhiḍhāna Mahā Nāyaka Sṭhayiraṇyan waḥanse wamha.

(Hippola Ḍhamma Rakkhita Sɔbhiṭābhiḍhāna, High Priest of the Malwaṭta Vihare at Kandy.

(Sd.) HIPPOLA

Mahanuwara Asgiri vihārāḍhipaṭi Yatawattē Chanḍajoṭṭyabhiḍhana Mahā Nāyaka Sthavirayan wahanse wamha—(Yatawattō Chanḍajoṭṭyābhiḍhana, High Priest of Asgiri Vihare at Kandy).

(Sd.) YATAWATTE

Hikkaduwe Srī Sumangala Sripāḍasthane saha Kolamba palate praḍhāna Nāyaka Sṭhavirayo (Hikkaduwe Srī Sumangala, High Priest of Adam's Peak and the District of Colombo).

(Sd.) H. SUMANGALA

Maligawe Prāchīna Pusṭakālāyaḍhyakshaka Surīyagoda Sonuṭṭara Sthavirayo (Surīyagoda Sonuṭṭara, Librarian of the Oriental Library at the Temple of the Tooth Relic at Knady).

(Sd.) S. SONUTTARA

Sugaṭa Sāsanadhaja Vinayā chāriya Ḍhammalankārābhiḍhana Nāyaka Sāhavira.

(Sd.) W. ḌHAMMALANKARA

Pawara neruttikā chariya Mahā Vibhavi Subhuti of Waskaduwa.

(Sd.) W. SUBHUTI

JAPAN

Accepted as included within the body of Northern Buḍḍhism.

Shaku Genyu	(Shingon Shu)
Fukuda Nichiyo	(Nichiren „)
Sanada Seyko	(Zen „)
Ito Quan Shyu	(„ „)
Takehana Hakuyo	(Jodo „)
Kono Rioshin	(Ji-Shu „)
Kiro Ki-ko	(Jodo Seizan„)
Harutani Shinsho	(Tendhi „)
Manabe Shun-myo	(Shingon „)

CHITTAGONG

Accepted for the Buḍḍhists of Chittagong.

Nagawa Parvaṭa Vihārāḍhipaṭi

Guna Megu Wini-Lankara,
Harbing, Chittagong, Bengal.